BLOOM

50 Things to Say, Think and Do with Anxious, Angry, and Over-the-Top Kids

Lynne Kenney, Psy.D. and
Wendy Young, LMSW, BCD

UNHOOKED BOOKS
An Imprint of High Conflict Institute Press
Scottsdale, Arizona

Publisher's Note

This publication is designed to provide accurate and authoritative information about the subject matters covered. It is sold with the understanding that neither the authors nor publisher are rendering mental health, legal, medical or other professional services or advice, either directly or indirectly. If expert assistance, counseling, or legal services are needed, the services of a competent professional should be sought. Neither the authors nor the publisher shall be liable or responsible for any loss or damage allegedly arising as a consequence of your use or application of any information or suggestions in this book.

Copyright © 2015 by Lynne Kenney and Wendy Young

Unhooked Books, LLC
7701 E. Indian School Rd., Ste. F
Scottsdale, AZ 85251

unhookedbooks.com

ISBN: 978-1-936268-82-5
eISBN: 978-1-936268-83-2

Cover design by Gordan Blazevik
Interior design by Kristen Onesti & Elle Phillips

Printed in the United States of America

PRAISE FOR BLOOM: 50 THINGS TO SAY, THINK AND DO WITH ANGRY, ANXIOUS AND OVER-THE-TOP KIDS

"When we change our own thinking, words and behavior, our children will do the same. This inspiring and must-read book demonstrates how. It helps make your parenting experience less stressful and develop a closer relationship with your child."

—**Jacek Debiec**, M.D., Ph.D., Child and Adolescent Psychiatrist, Neuroscientist, Assistant Professor at the University of Michigan, author of The Emotional Brain Revisited.

"As parents, we set the sensory, emotional and behavioral tone in our families. But when things get heated, sometimes we're not sure how to respond. With Bloom, we learn about the neurobiological underpinnings of our children's behavior so that we can stop reacting and instead respond with compassion."

—**Melissa Taylor** is a freelance writer, an award-winning educational blogger at Imagination Soup, an award-winning teacher with a M.A. in Education, and a mom of two children, ages 10 and 13.

"Practical, helpful, gentle, realistic, effective -- all of these describe this truly excellent book for parents and educators. Using these strategies will absolutely change your family for the better!"

—**James T. Webb**, Ph.D., author of A Parent's Guide to Gifted Children.

"Bloom is the practical social-emotional resource school psychologists have been waiting for. With printable mantras we can share with parents and teachers, I see all of our classrooms blooming!"

—**Rebecca Comizio**, M.A.-Ed, M.A., NCSP Nationally Certified School Psychologist and former English teacher.

"In heated situations, we need techniques to soothe our anxious child readily available so that we can stop yelling and start collaborating. By modeling behaviors we wish to see in our children, they will begin to flourish in a calmer and more compassionate environment. Bloom is the perfect option for time-starved parents who need answers now; a reference book you will refer to time and again."

—**Lisa Conrad**, B.A. Sociology, "Providing support for parents of gifted children" http://giftedparentingsupport.blogspot.com/

"Bloom is a relationship-changer!"

—**Michele Borba**, Ed.D., author of The Big Book of Parenting Solutions

"There are thousands of parenting books out there but there is only one with printable mantra cards that will rescue your relationships and transform your family life."

—**Sue Atkins**, author of Parenting Made Easy

"As a parent of three children, all with different temperaments, reading Bloom, I see mantras that suit each of our children's distinct personalities. Choose your favorite mantra, hang it on your fridge or in your car, use it for a week and watch how your relationships with your children grow."

—**Janet M. Patterson**, LCSW, MFT, and mom of triplets.

"Gentle, practical, and optimistic. Bloom offers parents do-able ways to teach children essential life skills."

—**Eileen Kennedy-Moore**, PhD, professor of The Great Courses video series, Raising Emotionally and Socially Healthy Kids.

"In Bloom, Lynne Kenney and Wendy Young have integrated neuroscience with psychology, blending the heart and science of best parenting practices! Their constructive mantras are a lifesaver for the overwhelmed parent just trying his or her best. A transformative resource unlike any other!"

—**Beth Onufrak**, PhD. Clinical Child Psychologist & Voice America Host of Child Psych Central: Discover the KidBrain; DrBethKids.com

"For 20 years we teachers have been stuck with time-out and exclusion as the most common forms of behavior management. With Bloom we finally have a new way. One that looks at the whole child and helps children behave for a lifetime not just for a moment."

—**Sue Milano,** MS, Educational Resource Specialist and Parenting Consultant

"BLOOM is a unique and beautiful guide that provides valuable insights that the hearts and brains of caring parents desire."

—**Deborah McNelis,** M.Ed. Founder Brain Insights, and author of The Brain Development Series Brain Insights ~ Basics to Brilliance!

CONTENTS

Will Teaching My Child To Be More Skillful Really Work?...................... 4

What You Will Find In This Book 7

How To Use This Book... 7

Intense Children Are Like Flowers In Your Garden
Not All Flowers Are Created Equal 9

Chapter 1: AM Mayhem
Happier Mornings Makeover 13

Chapter 2: Room Rehab
You Gotta "See It" To Take Action On It 29

Chapter 3: A Bit on Biting
Adieu to Toothy Troubles.. 43

Chapter 4: Aggression Alley
Help for Hitting... and Beyond 65

Chapter 5: Daunting Disrespect
The Sass is The Sauce.. 81

Chapter 6: Tell, Don't Yell
Calming the Chaos... 99

Chapter 7: Perpetual Motion
Busy Bodies Need To Move... 123

Chapter 8: Schoolhouse Blues
Better Behavior Blueprint.. 151

Chapter 9: Tearful Goodbyes
Smoother Separations... 169

Chapter 10: Trauma
When Pain Drives Behavior.. 187

Chapter 11: Children and Grief
An Early Mourning... 209

So Long, For Now 228

More Resources for You.. 228

A NOTE FROM WENDY AND LYNNE

We are so grateful you are here with us today. Bloom has been a long journey for us and we are pleased to share where we have arrived after years of contemplation.

We didn't start out parenting our own children the Bloom way. Nor did we know enough to share with our clients the Bloom perspective, until about 15 years ago. We bought into the popular consequence-based parenting philosophies until we saw that they were not working, particularly with our more anxious, angry and intense children. In many ways, it was our own children and the children with whom we worked that brought us to this more mindful place.

Therefore, with the deepest gratitude, we thank our husbands, children and families for helping us to find more peaceful loving hearts as parents and spouses. We also thank the thousands of families with whom we have worked who educated us, informed us and trusted us.

We hope that the real-life practical language on the following pages will inspire you to love more deeply and be present more often. Yet we know, first hand, it takes time.

With gratitude to all,

Wendy and Lynne

BLOOM

50 things to say, think and do with anxious, angry and over-the-top kids

If you are parenting angry, anxious or over-the-top kids, you've come to the right place. When our children live with intensity we are often confused about what to say and do to help them in the moment, right then. We often feel as though we should be able to control our children better when they are anxious, in a tantrum or being disrespectful.

Sometimes we receive feedback or even judgment from friends and family members who think we should be more strict or aggressive with our children to manage them better. This results in getting caught in The Discipline Trap, sending our children to time-out, telling them too forcefully to "stop" something and yelling when they misbehave. We've come to rely on techniques that give us the illusion of control. We have learned to value short-term compliance over long-term gains. The problem is, we find ourselves having to use these techniques over and over again, because they do little to teach our children more effective ways to handle things on their own. Our children (and we) suffer because of it. But there is a better way, the Bloom Way. Bloom Parenting changes everything.

Bloom helps you focus on building social-emotional skills within your relationship with your child to help you become a parent who is loving, kind, calm, and mature. Perhaps your plan was to raise children who are warm and wonderful adults. Yet the ins and outs of your daily experience when combined with your child's temperament, can leave you overwhelmed and exhausted causing you to say and do things you promised you never would. For parents like you, we've created Bloom Parenting, a new approach to human relationships that will change the way you perceive, think and feel about parenting, love, work and life.

BLOOM

A flourishing, healthy condition; the time or moment of greatest beauty, artistry, and creation. When given the proper conditions, it is what every flower does, bloom. So, too, does every child. Imagine with us, a loving world where every child reaches optimal growth, so he (or she) can realize his full potential. In Bloom, you will find the words, thoughts and actions to raise children who thrive and blossom.

Bloom focuses on providing you and your children with the words and actions you all need to develop better cognitive, social and emotional skills without punishment.

Bloom helps you put strategies in place to calm intensity, anger and anxiety so that your children become more competent and skillful with better communication, thinking and behavioral skills.

Bloom introduces language within your family that communicates, "Together we can solve this."

Bloom helps you use words and actions to calm feelings, leading to better mood management within your family.

Bloom helps you create a peaceful space between you and your child where you safely explore thoughts and feelings, offering new ways to think and behave.

Bloom helps you to feel less frustrated (or shamed) by your child's misbehavior by understanding the meaning of the behavior.

Bloom helps you understand how your child's brain functions during grief and trauma to help you help your child metabolize his or her feelings instead of becoming stuck in them.

Bloom is less concerned with instant compliance and more concerned with building a connection that fosters emotional stability.

Bloom helps you shift your thought-processes so that everyone in your family can grow, evolve, and effectively problem-solve to handle life's most difficult moments.

Bloom focuses on providing the solid foundational skills that will serve your child across his or her lifespan.

WILL TEACHING MY CHILD TO BE MORE SKILLFUL REALLY WORK?

We can guess what you might be thinking right now: "Sure. Sounds great on paper, this brave new world. In the meantime, I have tantrums, biting, grief and hitting with which to deal. I'll read this book later. After my kids are all grown up, maybe. Right now, I need a proven approach to deal with these behaviors."

We are right there with you! With seven children between the two of us as well as the thousands of kids we have seen in our practices, we may have seen it all. And Bloom works for about every problem we have ever come across. It is particularly useful with high intensity kids, the children for whom most traditional parenting techniques often fall short.

KEEPING IT REAL WITH BLOOM

Real parents with real problems, that's for whom Bloom is written. Throughout this book, you will read questions about behavioral challenges posed by real parents, like you. We will explore situations from toddlers to tweens. Bloom will provide you with the words, thoughts and actions you can use, one sentence at a time, to get to the heart of what skills your child needs to develop better cognitive, social, emotional, and behavioral management. Interacting with high-intensity children requires a calm approach, so we'll even give you the thoughts you can use as mantras when the going gets tough.

We have found this two-pronged approach, changing our own thoughts, while we support new skill-development for our children, is one of the most effective ways to lasting behavior change, and one that provides a path to a calm, peaceful family.

ARE YOU READY TO BECOME A BEHAVIORAL DETECTIVE?

With Bloom, we step back from the intensity of the moment and observe behavior by becoming "behavioral detectives." This allows us to understand what thoughts and feelings lay underneath our child's behavior. When we take the time to understand the needs behind our child's behavior we are able to provide new thoughts, words and actions our child can use to be more skillful. These new skills translate into improved behaviors, reducing the need for consequences or punishment.

HELP YOUR CHILDREN THINK ABOUT HOW THEY FEEL

What we think about and how we think influences, not only our behavior, but also our social relationships, academics and health. With Bloom we help our children develop critical thinking skills so they choose their thoughts more and are controlled by their thoughts less.

We also show you how to help your children understand their feelings. Most of us do not understand that our brain perceives environmental stimuli first, then we think about or try to understand our sensations and perceptions, which ultimately leads to our feelings. Helping children understand how they are interpreting social experiences, academic learning and the behavior of themselves, and others gives them the power to feel differently about life experiences.

"I hate math" can become, "I'm getting better at fractions." "I feel hurt," can become, "I'll tell my dad I feel ignored." "That makes me angry," can become "I am afraid, not really mad." Bloom raises children with better thinking skills who can identify **how what they think impacts how they feel,** so they are empowered to choose new behaviors.

BLOOM IS A WAY OF LIFE

There are many valuable parenting books available on the market. Many of them help you figure out ways to encourage your child to do the "right thing." The challenge is they focus on behavior as though it is always willful. What we see in our practices are children who wish to behave better but they are at a loss for what to think, say and do to effect a better outcome in the moment. As a society, we have relied on a type of back-and-forth dance with our children for decades. "Do as I say, or this will happen." It seems straightforward enough. Yet, some critical steps are missing in that approach. Bloom fills in the gaps, by bringing together the essential elements that converge to grow great kids: Empathy, attunement, skill building, and personal responsibility. When you adopt and then teach the new thoughts, words and actions, you are able to respond with love and kindness in moments that used to inspire anger or negativity.

One important thing we need to provide high-intensity children (as well as ourselves) is the opportunity to practice again and again, in a loving way. The wide array of "things to think, say and do" allows you to address complicated situations again and again with new skills not punishment.

WITH BLOOM, YOU AND YOUR CHILD ARE ON THE SAME TEAM

Bloom puts you squarely in your child's corner. With Bloom, you are both on the same side. There is no competition regarding who is right or wrong. It is simple, uncomplicated, and a thing of beauty, once achieved. Peace grows in children when there is equilibrium between what they need and what we, as parents provide.

Sunshine is to flowers what skill-building is to kids. So, You Ask, "Where do the Blooms come in?"

Flowers require sunshine, water, and soil to grow. As the gardeners of our families we need to plant seeds that will grow to raise happy skillful children. Sometimes what appears on the surface is not at all what your child needs you to attend to. Often it is what is below the surface, in the soil that needs help, nurturance and love. Whether it is watering the soil, digging out the bugs or pruning the flowers, Bloom helps us think more and dig deeper to help our children grow.

> When you are mindfully present and available to your child, even during the rough spots your behavior says: Together we can find solutions to challenges we face, each and every day.

WHAT YOU WILL FIND IN THIS BOOK

Answering real questions posed by parents like you, we explore common challenges families face every day. From biting and hitting to trouble learning, we practice the conversations and actions designed to raise ethical children from the inside out not just well-managed children from the outside in.

Each chapter is a new situation. The strategies and solutions provided are ideas, like a springboard for your own conversations and experiences. We hope you will use the Bloom strategies provided here to build your own version of Bloom. For some families the words may be just perfect, but other families will wish to alter the words to suit their needs. We encourage this.

HOW TO USE THIS BOOK

As busy parents, we understand that sometimes you need help in the moment, but you do not have a lot of time to read and sort through parenting strategies. Therefore, we have written a book that is designed to be "edible" meaning that you can digest small pieces in just a minute or so.

What separates Bloom from some of the other great parenting books you have read, is that in each chapter we have provided you and your child with printables of thoughts, words and actions you can take and even improve to manage the sticky moments without anger, in a more skillful manner.

Each of the printables is a mantra card that you are invited to copy, cut up and post on your fridge, in your bathroom, in your wallet, wherever you feel you need the tools to use in tough moments. You can also download and print them from our websites. You can choose the sentences or actions that best suit you and your family and use them one at a time. We have also provided you with blank cards to write in the thoughts, feelings and actions you and your family have developed, so that they suit you.

We consider these sentences or mantras the core feature of Bloom as parents have said to us over and over again, "I know what I am saying is not helping but I am not sure what to say, think or do."

Feel free to copy the specific mantras that suit you and even share them with teachers, other family members and professionals with whom your child works. One family we know copied and cut the pages and then laminated relevant mantras. The parents made sets of cards on binder rings and shared them, so that the teachers, parents and grandparents were using similar words as they helped their child along.

Make the thoughts, sentences and ideas on the printable pages your own, shape, change and improve them to suit your own personality. Bloom parenting is flexible, dynamic and growth-oriented. Bloom allows for creativity. Bloom can evolve with you as your children grow to meet the needs of each family member.

You may see some of the "What to Say, Think and Do" printable cards have some overlap. This is for very good reason. Some of the mantras work for various issues because they appeal to the same part of the brain. These sentences are provided on more than one occasion, not to be redundant, but because of the way in which this book is intended to be used.

As a parent, teacher, family member or care provider, you may read this book sequentially, or pick it up and use it "on the fly" when dealing with challenging behaviors. When it is used in the latter circumstance, we want to make sure the reader has access to all of the interventions that apply. When these mantras are used on a regular basis, they will become part of your natural way of responding to behavioral challenges.

The Table of Contents can guide you to specific chapter topics that interest you. While the situations we explore are from toddlers to school-agers, the strategies in this book can be applied across many different circumstances and age ranges.

The basic Bloom Parenting Method is about building cognitive, social and behavioral skill sets instead of using consequences and punishment to manage behavior. Read on... enjoy and help your children blossom.

Intense
Children Are
Like Flowers In
Your Garden

NOT ALL FLOWERS ARE CREATED EQUAL

They aren't all Zinnias. Zinnias are said to be amongst the easiest of flowers to grow. They require little care and maintenance, yet they continue to produce beautiful blossoms. One could literally throw a handful of seeds into the soil, walk away and find flowers growing in a short while, provided there is a bit of rain. Roses, on the other hand, require pruning, fertilizing, the right growing space, temperature and water to thrive. They, too, are beautiful, but require so much more care. The first thing a good gardener must do is recognize whether they have a Zinnia or a Rose.

WATER FLOWERS, NOT WEEDS

Are you paying attention to the numerous infractions your child engages in? There is a principle that says, "Whatever you pay attention to, you get more of!" Make sure you are watering the flowers, not the weeds. Do you want more misbehavior or more on track behavior? The answer to that question will tell you which behaviors to give your full attention and excitement to.

THE STINKY STUFF MATTERS, TOO

You knew we couldn't avoid it. Fertilizer, manure, whatever you call it, stinks. It makes us turn our noses up and grimace. Some behavior stinks, too. That's not all bad. Let the stinky behavior remind you of manure and help you kick into high gear when it comes to tending to your child. Behavior that stinks tells us that we need to pour more love, understanding, patience and skill-building into our children. It's a built-in warning system of sorts that says, "Hey, look here. I could use a little support around this!"

If a flower is wilting, we don't pluck it out of the garden, we give it a little water and TLC and bring it back to a thing of beauty. Sometimes our kids need a little "perking" up, too. Harsh words and looks of disdain do little to perk up a flower. We have yet to see them work on changing the behavior of children, either.

DOWN AND DIRTY

In gardening, soil is one very important factor. Having a properly nourished soil is the place from which the nutrients will be sourced and absorbed. Good gardeners make sure their soil is in tip-top condition prior to planting. Serious gardeners take samples of their soil and have it analyzed to see if everything is in balance (minerals, organic matter, aeration, water). If it's not, they go about getting things back to a more stable position.

DON'T BE "BAMBOOZLED" BY YOUR CHILD'S BEHAVIOR

If you feel as if you are doing everything right and your child's behavior still appears to be stuck in a slow pattern of growth, take heart. Remain encouraged and continue to keep calm and stay the course. Gardeners don't stop watering plants if they haven't flowered in one or two weeks. They know that in order to someday see that gorgeous bud, they must continue to water and care for the plant. They do this day after day, because the promise of that beautiful bloom is worth all of the effort they expend on a daily basis.

Still not convinced? Look no further than the Chinese bamboo plant. It may provide just the nudge you need to plow ahead, undaunted by a perceived lack of growth. When Chinese bamboo is planted, it appears to be dormant. The farmer cares for it and tends to it, only to see nothing.

He continues on in year two, with fertilizing, watering and tending. Still, he sees nothing. The farmer might be tempted to give up and hang up his watering can by year three or four, when still, nothing seems to be happening. Not an inch of growth. *Enter year five. This same bamboo plant, the one which didn't move an inch, may shoot up 80 feet or more in one growing season.*

While the farmer toiled and tended, the bamboo appeared to do nothing. It showed no signs of outward growth. Then, in one quick season, it grows to monumental proportions. To non-farmer types, it may have appeared that nothing happened for four years. Much to the contrary, that bamboo plant was working feverishly below the surface, setting down roots in preparation for a tremendous period of growth. Imagine what would have happened if the farmer gave up in year two, three or four! And so it goes with our children. When we fail to see change on the outside, we must remember the bamboo plant. An incredible amount may be going on beneath the surface. Keep watering, fertilizing and tending (or loving, embracing and believing)! Eventually, you will reap the fruits of your labor.

Let's get digging so your children begin blooming....

Hear more about how to use this
book directly from the authors

CHAPTER 1

AM
Mayhem

HAPPIER MORNINGS MAKEOVER

"Our mornings are all about me yelling at our kids (ages 6, 7 and 12), 'brush your teeth, comb your hair, and eat your breakfast'. It pains me to hear the words that come out of my mouth, 'What's taking you so long?' 'What's the matter with you? Hurry-up! You're so slow.' 'How many times do I have to ask you to put your shoes on?' We need clear strategies to help us get out the door without the stress."

Mornings are hectic for many families. Kids may dawdle and be slow to get dressed. Mom and Dad may be getting ready for work. Setting up routines that help children independently accomplish their morning tasks will limit the chaos, stop the yelling, and bring peace to your home.

We also need to make an effort to communicate face to face with our children in the morning. We cannot parent from the kitchen or the couch. Take the time to walk up to your children and give them direct instructions up close. Be personal, loving and clear. *If you are yelling from another room, "Get dressed!" You are not setting up the scene for a happy calm morning.*

Our children feel stressed, worried and scared when we are in the habit of rushing in the morning. This can make everyone defensive, angry or anxious.

WHAT CAN WE DO TO HELP?

As parents, we set the sensory, emotional and behavioral tone in our families. If we do not manage our time effectively, complete enough tasks the night before, or monitor our task lists, we are often rushed, forget things, and yell to get our kids moving. You can set the tone for a "soft entry" into the day's activities by managing your time well. Your own intensity impacts the moment. Are you feeling calm and prepared or rushed? We can slow down and feel better prepared by spending a few minutes each day to planning out what needs to be accomplished in order to begin the day peacefully.

On a day when you need to go to work early or the children have a day packed with activities, get everything ready the night before. That includes the items you will be taking to work, what the children will be taking to school and all of their changes in clothing or necessary equipment for their daily activities. The most common reason families feel rushed in the morning, is that they are left running around finding needed items right before trying to get out the door.

Transitions can be challenging for everyone. When you consider all the task demands the morning brings, it's common for families to feel stressed-out.

DEVELOP ROUTINES

Developing family systems and routines to get tasks accomplished is sure to help. Begin by sitting down with your children and having them write (or draw) out their morning, afternoon and evening routines on a marker board or sheet of card stock to hang on their bedroom doors. This provides your children with visible reminders of their "to-dos".

Next, make sure that your children have the tools for morning success readily available. Ask yourself, are my kid's clothes out and ready to put on when they first get up? Are the backpacks packed and by the door? Are the lunches made and ready-to-go? Take the time the evening before to help your children "prepare" for the next day by getting their things ready for a peaceful exit out the door.

Remember, routines are more than task lists. Building routines around eating well, sleeping and even doing homework all lead to more successful behavior. Keep in mind a rushed morning makes it more difficult for kids to do well and be happy in school. Kids need a good night's sleep, then a few hugs along with nutritious food to thrive. Feeding our children whole foods or even dinner for breakfast ensures they eat their fill of essential amino acids and healthy fats to sustain them throughout the day.

C-O-L-L-A-B-O-R-A-T-I-O-N IS KEY!

Anxious, angry and intense children often respond well to collaboration. They like to be part of the solution. One challenge is that they can be defensive when we speak with them because they have so much anxiety. So, take a deep breath, plan on remaining calm and be a partner not a dictator. In turn your children will learn that every conversation is not another "blaming moment" and find that collaborating helps them feel calm.

Collaborating with our children regarding the order of their morning routines and tasks encourages them to buy-in. Take the time to sit with your children and talk about what a successful day looks like. Help them learn to plan out a day filled with small specific accomplishments. Helping your children think about, discuss and imagine what a successful day looks like helps them to be better at organization, planning and task completion. The conversation may begin with thinking about routines but can generalize to better execution of other daily life skills as well.

Our kids want to be independent and skillful. They also want to please and spend time with us. We can raise skillful children by helping them learn to do for themselves what they are capable of and then rewarding them with our time, love and patience. While it may be easier (and tempting) to just complete certain tasks for our children, we do them a great disservice when we fall into this trap.

In addition to providing the skills to accomplish their morning tasks, your kids benefit from family time in the morning. Don't make it just about task lists. Spend a few moments, making breakfast together, folding the laundry, reading a book, singing a song or taking the dog on a walk. These moments of connection matter for a lifetime.

HERE ARE 5 SIMPLE WAYS TO MAKE MORNINGS LESS STRESSFUL

1. Create a clear written morning, afternoon and evening routine for each child. Write down their tasks in order, with their help, so that your children begin to develop an internal rhythm regarding task completion. It can really help if the task list is a picture schedule. Help your children draw or cut pictures out of magazines to make their own picture schedules.

> MY MORNING ROUTINE
>
> Get up and use the bathroom.
> Put on my clothes.
> Pick-up things on the floor of my bedroom and put them in their homes.
> Go to the kitchen for my brain food.
> Get out the door with a smile.

2. Wake up before your children in order to get dressed yourself. Let's face it, the whole shower, do your hair and get dressed process takes time. You need to build this time in before your children are up. Your morning routine is a model for your children's preparedness.

3. Before your children get up, prepare a healthy family breakfast, do a quick clean-up of anything left out the night before and create a welcoming morning environment for your family. Leaving for school or work with a well-organized house will make coming home at the end of the day a lot brighter.

4. Pack lunches and school snacks the night before. If your children are old enough to pack their own lunches, you can make this part of their evening routines. You might even choose to prepare paper bags or small boxes of nutritious snacks on Sunday evenings, so that your children can grab-n-go with ease.

5. Make backpack preparation a "night-before" task. Those permission slips, water bottles and homework are best ready-to-go by the back door before breakfast.

For more details on family systems and managing family routines, see **The Family Coach Method** by Dr. Kenney or **Tough Love: Proven strategies for raising confident, kind, resilient kids** by Lisa Stiepock and Amy Iorio. **The Confident Mom**, Susan Heid has a good daily planner for families.

IN A NUTSHELL: WHAT MAKES MORNINGS SO STRESSFUL?

The family needs a more consistent routine to keep things calm and orderly.

The routine needs to be visible (written, drawn, a chart) and reviewed/discussed/improved on a regular basis (5 minute morning wake-up meeting or 15 minute weekend family meeting.)

The family needs systems, "This is how we take care of our dog," "make sure the laundry is properly put away," "clean-up after dinner," etc.

The parents need to spend more time teaching the children how to accomplish specific tasks for greater independence.

One parent or child may be stuck in their emotional brain, spilling over instead of focusing on getting things done.

The children may have so much difficulty in school that homework is always left for the morning. Working with the teacher may be the ticket here.

The parents may have grown-up in a home that was too chaotic or too confining and they are still responding to the past in the present.

The family may not have consistent eating and sleeping routines leaving their bodies and minds tired and poorly fed.

A FEW FINAL WORDS...

Children rely on their parents to get their morning, afternoon and evening tasks accomplished. Yet kids can be more masterful and accountable when they know exactly what is expected. Consider the tasks of everyday living that each of your children can accomplish based on their age, skill sets and developmental level. Help your children experience morning success by being organized, helping them plan ahead, and creating multi-sensory opportunities for them to monitor and manage their morning activities.

WHAT YOU CAN **SAY**

What can I help you with this morning?

How can I help you feel refreshed and ready for the day?

Waking up late makes us hurry. We're going to work on getting up a bit earlier so we can have more time together.

Let's wake-up mindful and alert so that our brains and bodies are ready for today's accomplishments.

Today will be a bright day, when we return home we'll have so much to say. With a skip in our step and a smile on our face, we're ready for this day.

We want to begin our day with calm bodies and peaceful minds. Would you like me to come in and turn on your soft music to wake you up?

Today, we'll take the time to make breakfast together. Just spending time together in the morning, fills our hearts with peace.

If we work together and are efficient, we'll have time for outside play or a walk around the neighborhood.

Let's look at our picture schedule to see that we are on track.

We are doing great on our 'To Do' list! You can feel proud that you got your back-pack and lunch ready last night.

You can feel proud of yourself when your bed is made, your room is picked up and you accomplished your morning routine on your own.

We have some extra time this morning, would you like to play outside for a few minutes? I'll play as well.

We need to get out the door on time. Let's do it peacefully, one step at a time.

We can all help each other. We are a great team!

WHAT YOU CAN **THINK**

Beginning the day with mindfulness, focusing on being alertly in the present can lower our stress levels.

Stress causes hormones to surge, moving us into fight, flight or freeze, so my staying calm really matters.

I can focus on being better prepared, so the children are less rushed.

When I get myself ready before the children get up, I can be there to kindly help them stay on task.

I will focus on one task at a time and not overwhelm my children, with my own anxiety or frustration.

Rushing my children does not help them.

Rushing sets the tone for an anxious day.

We need to plan our mornings to be more efficient.

Helping our children take an active role in making mornings a success will teach them much needed skills for later in life.

I need to model being kind, respectful and calm every day.

I'm not striving for perfection. I'm aiming at being a good role model for our children.

We may make poor choices or say things we don't mean, because we're amped up. As a parent, I will choose not to over-respond.

My children want to have a reliable, calm parent.

When we all do our part, we are calm and relaxed.

WHAT YOU CAN **DO**

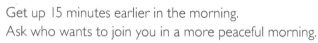

Get up 15 minutes earlier in the morning.
Ask who wants to join you in a more peaceful morning.

Shower or bathe the night before. Help your kids get in the habit of doing the same.

Wake-up with a "Be Calm Mindset." Embrace the intention of remaining peaceful, connected and loving.

Gather together as a family for five minutes to review your planners or checklists.

Go over your children's routine boards and compliment them on a job well done.

Make a list of brief activities you can do as a family when your morning routines are completed early.

If you have extra time help your children review for today's vocabulary, language or math tests.

Research shows that morning exercise can improve school grades so consider a 15-minute family walk, game of basketball or foursquare.

Find fast and free family activities in Rebecca Cohen's book *Fifteen Minutes Outside: 365 ways to get out of the house and connect with your kids.*

More tips from Lynne: Four Eye-Opening
Ways to Make Your Mornings Calmer

What can I help you with this morning?

BLOOM 50 Things To Say, Think, And Do With Anxious, Angry, and Over-the-Top Kids

How can I help you feel refreshed and ready for the day?

BLOOM 50 Things To Say, Think, And Do With Anxious, Angry, and Over-the-Top Kids

Waking up late makes us hurry. We're going to work on getting up a bit earlier so we can have more time together.

BLOOM 50 Things To Say, Think, And Do With Anxious, Angry, and Over-the-Top Kids

Let's wake-up mindful and alert so that our brains and bodies are ready for today's accomplishments.

BLOOM 50 Things To Say, Think, And Do With Anxious, Angry, and Over-the-Top Kids

Today will be a bright day, when we return home we'll have so much to say. With a skip in our step and a smile on our face, we're ready for this day.

BLOOM 50 Things To Say, Think, And Do With Anxious, Angry, and Over-the-Top Kids

We want to begin our day with calm bodies and peaceful minds.

BLOOM 50 Things To Say, Think, And Do With Anxious, Angry, and Over-the-Top Kids

SAY

Would you like me to come in and turn on your soft music to wake you up?

SAY

Today, we'll take the time to make breakfast together.

SAY

Just spending time together in the morning, fills our hearts with peace.

SAY

If we work together and are efficient, we'll have time for outside play or a walk around the neighborhood.

SAY

Let's look at our picture schedule to see that we are on track.

SAY

We are doing great on our 'To Do' list!

SAY

SAY

You can feel proud that you got your back-pack and lunch ready last night.

BLOOM 50 Things To Say, Think, And Do With Anxious, Angry, and Over-the-Top Kids

You can feel proud of yourself when your bed is made, your room is picked up and you accomplished your morning routine on your own.

BLOOM 50 Things To Say, Think, And Do With Anxious, Angry, and Over-the-Top Kids

THINK

Beginning the day with mindfulness, focusing on being alertly in the present can lower our stress levels.

BLOOM 50 Things To Say, Think, And Do With Anxious, Angry, and Over-the-Top Kids

THINK

Stress causes hormones to surge, moving us into fight, flight or freeze, so my staying calm really matters.

BLOOM 50 Things To Say, Think, And Do With Anxious, Angry, and Over-the-Top Kids

THINK

I can focus on being better prepared, so the children are less rushed.

BLOOM 50 Things To Say, Think, And Do With Anxious, Angry, and Over-the-Top Kids

THINK

When I get myself ready before the children get up, I can be there to kindly help them stay on task.

BLOOM 50 Things To Say, Think, And Do With Anxious, Angry, and Over-the-Top Kids

SAY

We have some extra time this morning, would you like to play outside for a few minutes? I'll play as well.

SAY

We need to get out the door on time. Let's do it peacefully, one step at a time.

SAY

We can all help each other. We are a great team!

THINK

Rushing my children does not help them.

THINK

Rushing sets the tone for an anxious day.

THINK

We need to plan our mornings to be more efficient.

THINK

Helping our children take an active role in making mornings a success will teach them much needed skills for later in life.

BLOOM 50 Things To Say, Think, And Do With Anxious, Angry, and Over-the-Top Kids

THINK

I need to model being kind, respectful and calm every day.

BLOOM 50 Things To Say, Think, And Do With Anxious, Angry, and Over-the-Top Kids

THINK

I'm not striving for perfection. I'm aiming at being a good role model for our children.

BLOOM 50 Things To Say, Think, And Do With Anxious, Angry, and Over-the-Top Kids

THINK

We may make poor choices or say things we don't mean, because we're amped up. As a parent, I will choose not to over-respond.

BLOOM 50 Things To Say, Think, And Do With Anxious, Angry, and Over-the-Top Kids

THINK

My children want to have a reliable, calm parent.

BLOOM 50 Things To Say, Think, And Do With Anxious, Angry, and Over-the-Top Kids

THINK

When we all do our part, we are calm and relaxed.

BLOOM 50 Things To Say, Think, And Do With Anxious, Angry, and Over-the-Top Kids

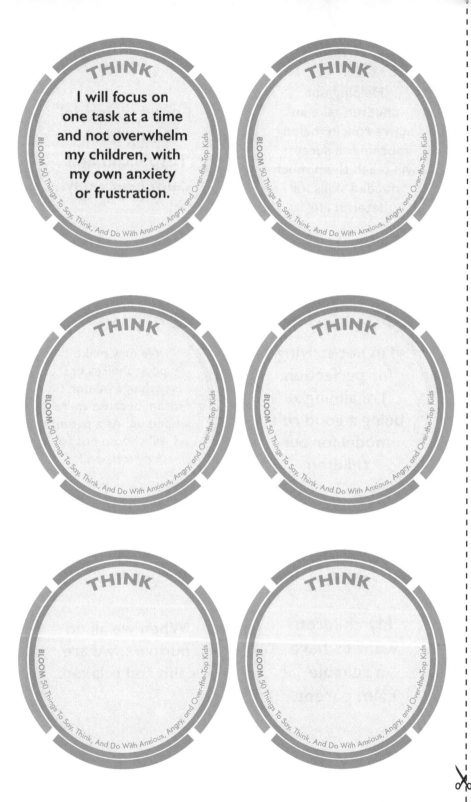

THINK

I will focus on one task at a time and not overwhelm my children, with my own anxiety or frustration.

BLOOM 50 Things To Say, Think, And Do With Anxious, Angry, and Over-the-Top Kids

THINK

BLOOM 50 Things To Say, Think, And Do With Anxious, Angry, and Over-the-Top Kids

THINK

BLOOM 50 Things To Say, Think, And Do With Anxious, Angry, and Over-the-Top Kids

THINK

BLOOM 50 Things To Say, Think, And Do With Anxious, Angry, and Over-the-Top Kids

THINK

BLOOM 50 Things To Say, Think, And Do With Anxious, Angry, and Over-the-Top Kids

THINK

BLOOM 50 Things To Say, Think, And Do With Anxious, Angry, and Over-the-Top Kids

DO

Get up
15 minutes earlier
in the morning.
Ask who wants
to join you in a
more peaceful
morning.

BLOOM 50 Things To Say, Think, And Do With Anxious, Angry, and Over-the-Top Kids

DO

Shower or bathe
the night before.
Help your kids get
in the habit of
doing the same.

BLOOM 50 Things To Say, Think, And Do With Anxious, Angry, and Over-the-Top Kids

DO

Wake-up with
a "Be Calm
Mindset." Embrace
the intention of
remaining peaceful,
connected
and loving.

BLOOM 50 Things To Say, Think, And Do With Anxious, Angry, and Over-the-Top Kids

DO

Gather together
as a family for
five minutes to
review your
planners
or checklists.

BLOOM 50 Things To Say, Think, And Do With Anxious, Angry, and Over-the-Top Kids

DO

Go over your
children's routine
boards and
compliment them
on a job
well done.

BLOOM 50 Things To Say, Think, And Do With Anxious, Angry, and Over-the-Top Kids

DO

Make a list of
brief activities
you can do as a
family when your
morning routines
are completed
early.

BLOOM 50 Things To Say, Think, And Do With Anxious, Angry, and Over-the-Top Kids

DO

If you have extra time help your children review for today's vocabulary, language or math tests.

BLOOM 50 Things To Say, Think, And Do With Anxious, Angry, and Over-the-Top Kids

DO

Research shows that morning exercise can improve school grades so consider a 15-minute family walk, game of basketball or foursquare.

BLOOM 50 Things To Say, Think, And Do With Anxious, Angry, and Over-the-Top Kids

DO

Find fast and free family activities in Rebecca Cohen's book *Fifteen Minutes Outside: 365 ways to get out of the house and connect with your kids.*

BLOOM 50 Things To Say, Think, And Do With Anxious, Angry, and Over-the-Top Kids

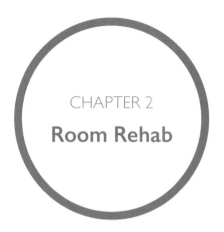

CHAPTER 2

Room Rehab

YOU GOTTA "SEE IT" TO TAKE ACTION ON IT

"My 9-year-old son has a hard time cleaning his room, without blowing up. It's like I'm asking him to pilot a rocket to the moon. He'll tell me he's confused about what goes where, even though I have shown him a hundred times. When I try to teach him once again, he gets furious. I can see he is suffering, how can I help?"

Most of us think of tasks of everyday living like cleaning the dishes, folding the laundry or cleaning one's room, in order from beginning to end. First, we do "this." Then next we do "that." This is helpful for children who think linearly, are able to remember and execute tasks in order and for those children who are supported by visual and verbal cuing (picture schedules, routine lists, and helpful parents).

But for many children particularly those with low frustration tolerance, a task like cleaning one's room is a reminder of how difficult daily activities can be. Helping children develop routines with *The End in Mind,* as Stephen Covey says, helps intense children learn to break bigger tasks into smaller pieces. Covey explains in *The Seven Habits of Highly Effective People*, that many people need to see or visualize what task completion looks like before they can execute it. "It is based on the principle that all things are created twice. There is a mental (first) creation, and a physical (second) creation. The physical creation follows the mental, just as a building follows a blueprint."

National speaker and speech therapist Sarah Ward, M.S. CCC-SLP echoed this sentiment, "Non-verbal memory, precedes verbal memory, so often children need to imagine what they will do before they can talk about it, then execute the vision." (Presentation Lexis Preparatory School, Scottsdale, Arizona January 17, 2013). This is one reason it's so helpful for children and adolescents to visualize what life will look like when the problem has less of a hold on them. Since anger and anxiety can interfere with thinking skills, making activities visual helps to calm your child's brain.

WHAT DOES IT LOOK LIKE?

Helping your child to visualize what a clean room will look like is a first step toward managing the overwhelm that leads to anger and frustration. Have a conversation, draw a picture or even have your son close his eyes and tell you what he sees as you walk him through the parts of cleaning a room.

"What will we see, when your room is clean?"

"What does a clean room look like?"

"What will the bed be like?"

"What will the floor look like?"

"What will someone see when they walk into the room?"

"Where will all the books be?"

"Where will your clothing be?"

"What will be on the chair?"

"What will be on the dresser?"

"What will be sitting on the floor?"

"What will be hanging in the closets?"

"How will we know when the room is clean?"

Remember, for many of our children tackling something like the morning routine, homework or tasks of daily living like cleaning your room feel HUGE and overwhelming. When we break down those tasks into parts (chunks) and we imagine what it will look and feel like (what will you see, how will you feel) to accomplish the task, kids feel less defensive, afraid, frustrated or angry.

In order to break the task down into smaller parts, you can draw three horizontal boxes on a sheet of paper and talk with your son about what he will tackle first, then next. We call this simple planning technique "Draw It Out." The three boxes represent the beginning, middle and end of any part (chunk) of a task or activity. You can then talk with your child about what they "Imagine" or "See" they will need to do to get from "Here" (the beginning) to "There" (the end). It is true, you might have four or five rows of boxes, depending on how big the task is. But your child will be better able to see what are the sequential parts of a much greater task. This will reduce overwhelm and improve your son's ability to complete the task one step (or box) at a time.

HOW YOU WILL GET "FROM HERE TO THERE"

You can also help your child, tween or teen develop an image of what they are trying to attain, by exploring the "Who, What, When, Where and How" of what is needed to "get from here to there." The concept of getting from here to there is helpful as it implies forward motion leading to task completion. Here are some prompts to help your conversation along.

WHO

"Who will help you clean your room?"

"Will you do it on your own?"

"Do you want me to help?"

WHAT

"What will you need to get from here to there?"

"What cleaning supplies will you need to clean your room?"

"What will you need to hang your clothes up in your closet?"

"What will you put where?"

"What is your plan for keeping your room clean?"

WHEN

"When will you clean your room?"

"Will you do certain tasks specific days, so the entire job feels easier?"

"What time and day will you tackle what parts of cleaning your room?"

"Will you break-down cleaning your room into chunks? Like throwing away old wrappers, food and things you no longer need first?"

"When choosing a home for each item, decide where everything lives."

WHERE

Every object needs a home, where will each item's home be?

Where will you put your shoes?

Where will you hang your pants?

Your wallet goes on your dresser, your socks go in the top left drawer, your volleyball shoes go on the bottom shelf in your closet etc.

HOW

Let's draw out what the beginning, middle and end are for the story, "This is how I clean my room."

How will you begin cleaning your room?

How will you choose what to keep and what to throw away?

How often will you straighten up your room?

How will you maintain a clean room?

How can I help you?

WHAT YOU CAN **SAY**

I know it might feel like you always have chores to do.

Having a long to-do list can be aggravating.

It can feel frustrating having to clean your room.

Sometimes, getting started is the hardest part. Once you're started, it gets a lot easier!

It would be fun if your room would clean itself.

Learning how to take care of our spaces and things is an important part of growing up.

Let's tackle one part of cleaning your room at a time, so that we can experience success.

It may feel like I am nagging you, but I am trying to help.

Approaching all tasks one piece at a time makes completing the task easier.

Once we learn how to imagine the who, what, when, where and how of completing a task, all tasks get easier.

Let's work for 20 minutes, then take a 10 minute break! I'll set the timer! Ready, set, GO!

WHAT YOU CAN **THINK**

Organization is a skill that some children and even adults, need to be taught.

Feeling overwhelmed by the enormity of a task is common for some children.

Breaking tasks down into smaller actionable bits is just the ticket.

I may need to approach tasks with my child a bit at a time, so he feels competent and skillful.

Sometimes what is easy for me is hard for others.

Helping my child imagine what success looks like, helps him make progress.

Sometimes we need more than words to execute tasks, we may need images, pictures or a written plan.

I can stay with my child while he accomplishes this task, just to let him feel my support.

From time to time, I can work along with him. I'll let him take the main responsibility for this task, though.

WHAT YOU CAN **DO**

Take the time to explore the who, what, when, where and how questions with your son, maybe not all at once.

Even one "How will we do it," "What will our plan be," "Where will we begin," question can be a new way of approaching a task for your son. Know that learning how to tackle big projects is a necessary life skill.

Remember that avoidance, anger or frustration, are signs that your son doesn't feel skillful or is feeling overwhelmed.

Most of us would rather our rooms clean themselves, your son is not alone in this. Find the humor in it and be playful about it.

Draw an imaginary line down the middle of the room (or use painter's tape) and challenge your child to see which side of the room he can clean faster. Let him guess how long each side will take and see how close he comes. Take a break between each side. Don't forget to say, "On your mark, get set, go!" Create some fanfare and fun!

It may take effort over time to clean the room and maintain it, try to stay calm and know that focusing on discrete parts of the task without anger leads best to skill development.

Be prepared to help your son with this and other tasks on an ongoing basis.

Make sure you do the task with your son, not for him. If we always do our kid's tasks they never learn how to do them themselves.

Teach your child how to develop a "plan" before he takes action. Help your son "think out" the steps to task completion. Create a task list together with your son and provide him an "official clipboard", so he can check off tasks as they are done. Some kids are motivated by seeing their progress on paper.

IN CLOSING

This chapter has been about cleaning one's room, but you can see that helping your child see what their "end game" would *look like* applies to many everyday situations and common life experiences. Providing your children with the skills to preview, plan, problem-solve, and practice builds smarter, more capable kids. It is valuable to note that when you teach your children how to "think things out" and "prepare a plan" you are enhancing their thinking skills and executive function. These skills are important life skills needed for home, school and social success.

Remember, anger and frustration erupt because tasks feel so large they are insurmountable. Teaching your children to break tasks down and do one part at a time leads to a feeling of accomplishment instead of overwhelm.

More tips from Lynne: Clean Your Room
and Other Tales of Chore Resistance

I know it might feel like you always have chores to do.

BLOOM 50 Things To Say, Think, And Do With Anxious, Angry, and Over-the-Top Kids

Having a long to-do list can be aggravating.

BLOOM 50 Things To Say, Think, And Do With Anxious, Angry, and Over-the-Top Kids

It can feel frustrating having to clean your room.

BLOOM 50 Things To Say, Think, And Do With Anxious, Angry, and Over-the-Top Kids

Sometimes, getting started is the hardest part. Once you're started, it gets a lot easier!

BLOOM 50 Things To Say, Think, And Do With Anxious, Angry, and Over-the-Top Kids

It would be fun if your room would clean itself.

BLOOM 50 Things To Say, Think, And Do With Anxious, Angry, and Over-the-Top Kids

Learning how to take care of our spaces and things is an important part of growing up.

BLOOM 50 Things To Say, Think, And Do With Anxious, Angry, and Over-the-Top Kids

SAY

Let's tackle
one part of cleaning
your room at
a time, so that
we can experience
success.

SAY

It may feel like
I am nagging you,
but I am trying
to help.

SAY

Approaching all
tasks one piece
at a time makes
completing the
task easier.

SAY

Once we learn
how to imagine the
who, what, when,
where and how of
completing a task,
all tasks get
easier.

SAY

Let's work for
20 minutes, then
take a 10 minute
break! I'll set
the timer!
Ready, set, GO!

SAY

THINK

Organization is a skill that some children and even adults, need to be taught.

THINK

Feeling overwhelmed by the enormity of a task is common for some children.

THINK

Breaking tasks down into smaller actionable bits is just the ticket.

THINK

I may need to approach tasks with my child a bit at a time, so he feels competent and skillful.

THINK

Sometimes what is easy for me is hard for others.

THINK

Helping my child imagine what success looks like, helps him make progress.

THINK

Sometimes we need more than words to execute tasks, we may need images, pictures or a written plan.

BLOOM 50 Things To Say, Think, And Do With Anxious, Angry, and Over-the-Top Kids

THINK

I can stay with my child while he accomplishes this task, just to let him feel my support. From time to time, I can work along with him. I'll let him take the main responsibility for this task, though.

BLOOM 50 Things To Say, Think, And Do With Anxious, Angry, and Over-the-Top Kids

THINK

BLOOM 50 Things To Say, Think, And Do With Anxious, Angry, and Over-the-Top Kids

THINK

BLOOM 50 Things To Say, Think, And Do With Anxious, Angry, and Over-the-Top Kids

THINK

BLOOM 50 Things To Say, Think, And Do With Anxious, Angry, and Over-the-Top Kids

THINK

BLOOM 50 Things To Say, Think, And Do With Anxious, Angry, and Over-the-Top Kids

DO

Take the time to explore the who, what, when, where and how questions with your son, maybe not all at once.

BLOOM 50 Things To Say, Think, And Do With Anxious, Angry, and Over-the-Top Kids

DO

Even one "How will we do it," "What will our plan be," "Where will we begin," question can be a new way of approaching a task for your son.

BLOOM 50 Things To Say, Think, And Do With Anxious, Angry, and Over-the-Top Kids

DO

Know that learning how to tackle big projects is a necessary life skill.

BLOOM 50 Things To Say, Think, And Do With Anxious, Angry, and Over-the-Top Kids

DO

Remember that avoidance, anger or frustration, are signs that your son doesn't feel skillful or is feeling overwhelmed.

BLOOM 50 Things To Say, Think, And Do With Anxious, Angry, and Over-the-Top Kids

DO

Most of us would rather our rooms clean themselves, your son is not alone in this. Find the humor in it and be playful about it.

BLOOM 50 Things To Say, Think, And Do With Anxious, Angry, and Over-the-Top Kids

DO

Draw an imaginary line down the middle of the room and challenge your child to see which side of the room he can clean faster. Let him guess how long each side will take and see how close he comes. Don't forget to say, "On your mark, get set, go!"

BLOOM 50 Things To Say, Think, And Do With Anxious, Angry, and Over-the-Top Kids

DO

It may take effort over time to clean the room and maintain it, focus on discrete parts of the task leads best to skill development.

BLOOM 50 Things To Say, Think, And Do With Anxious, Angry, and Over-the-Top Kids

DO

Be prepared to help your son with this and other tasks on an ongoing basis.

BLOOM 50 Things To Say, Think, And Do With Anxious, Angry, and Over-the-Top Kids

DO

Make sure you do the task with your son, not for him. If we always do our kid's tasks they never learn how to do them themselves.

BLOOM 50 Things To Say, Think, And Do With Anxious, Angry, and Over-the-Top Kids

DO

Teach your child how to develop a "plan" before he takes action.

BLOOM 50 Things To Say, Think, And Do With Anxious, Angry, and Over-the-Top Kids

DO

Help your son "think out" the steps to task completion.

BLOOM 50 Things To Say, Think, And Do With Anxious, Angry, and Over-the-Top Kids

DO

Create a task list together provide an "official clipboard", so he can check off tasks as they are done. Some kids are motivated by seeing their progress on paper.

BLOOM 50 Things To Say, Think, And Do With Anxious, Angry, and Over-the-Top Kids

CHAPTER 3
A Bit on Biting

ADIEU TO TOOTHY TROUBLES

"We cannot get through a play date without my almost three-year-old biting our one-year-old. It's embarrassing. I separate the kids when one of them bites and as soon as they are back to play, our older son is back to biting. The other parents don't want us to attend playgroup anymore, because it's always a disaster. I spoke with our doctor. She said to use vinegar. Someone else recommended that I bite back. What do you think? Should I try that? Sigh."

WE'RE SO HAPPY YOU ASKED!

Biting is one of the ways in which kids communicate when they don't yet have the words to express themselves. Biting causes strong emotions in many adults. Parents of biters are often embarrassed and upset. When parents understand why children bite, as well as how to properly deal with it, things become much easier for everyone involved.

WHAT MAKES KIDS BITE?

Biting seems like the quickest way to get the point across. The biter may be frustrated, mad, or overwhelmed. Not yet having the verbal skills, or cognitive ability to process all this and put it into words, it's no wonder that biting is one of the big concerns in the early years. Biting can also be a sign of sensory under-stimulation, some kids seek oral feedback to calm or even energize their brains. These kids can often benefit from occupational therapy. As a parent, teacher or clinician you may enjoy the work of Dr. Lucy Jane Miller, author of *Sensational Kids*.

Remember, your child doesn't have the maturity or skills to relax, take a deep breath, and express his frustration like an older child. These skills take time and require a patient, nurturing parent, teacher or caregiver to convey and model these abilities. The keys are to teach language, communication and mood modulation skills to your little ones.

IN A NUTSHELL: WHY KIDS BITE.

1. They do not have the language, words or ability to express what they need to say.

2. They are frustrated, upset or irritated, and biting seems to be the quickest way for them to communicate this.

3. The child is overwhelmed by sensory input when several other children are present.

4. Even though the child "knows" biting hurts on a cognitive level, he may not have developed the emotional maturity to control this urge when frustrated.

5. At a young age, biting is normal and needs to be redirected.

6. The child may be in need of more empathy, touch, or understanding, and is expressing this through biting.

7. The child is impulsive and unable to resist his urges.

8. The child is teething, having oral sensory issues or seeking oral pressure.

> While it's shocking and probably embarrassing when your child bites, it's not unusual behavior for young kids. When children are overcome with feelings such as anger, fear, frustration or disappointment, for example, because another child has possession of a toy they want, they don't have the language to express it. You help the child by stating how he might feel and providing him with the solutions (new words, thoughts and behaviors) the child cannot find on his own. It's important to help the child figure out, what thought, feeling or perception caused their escalation because awareness provides the opportunity to make a different choice next time.

Talking things out, instead of punishing, teaches positive actions. Let's explore how you could do that.

HOW DO I "TALK IT OUT" WITH MY CHILD?

Throughout Bloom, you will hear us discuss how important it is to have non-threatening explorations with your child about experiences in order to help him develop new words, thoughts and behaviors to manage difficult situations better. What we tend to do with our children when either they are upset or we are upset is respond by either telling them what not to do, as in "Knock that off!" or by disengaging from the situation by telling them to go somewhere else, "That's it, you're in time-out!"

If we can breathe and develop the habit of empathizing with and validating our children's feelings before we take any other action we can help them to develop better internal self-regulation skills while improving their ability to problem solve at the same time.

When you are building your child's thinking and social-emotional skills the best time to have the conversation is when your child is calm enough to talk it out.

When we meet with parents and teachers we explore the fact that there are essentially three times when you can intervene. We call them "MOMENTS."

MOMENT 1: The first is prior to the escalation or incident (this is our preference).

MOMENT 2: The second is during the incident.

MOMENT 3: The third is after the full-blown escalation or incident.

Then we teach the parents and teachers The Bloom "Manage the Moment" Method. We help them examine misbehaviors by examining what MOMENT they were in when they chose to help or intervene. Knowing what MOMENT you are in impacts what you think, say and do.

Consider this, most of us wait until MOMENT 3 the challenge has taken place to "do something." Yet, at this point your child's cortisol and adrenaline are running so your main role is to help your child calm down. The conversation and skill building then takes place when your child is calm enough to attend without feeling angry or defensive. Since in this example, we missed the opportunity to work in MOMENT 1, intervening early to prevent the escalation and biting, let's look at what happens in MOMENTS 2 and 3, just after the biting has taken place and a few minutes later (or sometimes hours later depending on the level of emotional arousal) when it's time to circle back and teach new skills.

In the moment of the transgression (MOMENT 2), you may wonder, "What do I do now?" "I need to show the other parents, I take this seriously and my child needs to be punished." Yet, punishment is not the answer. In fact, this may be a time of high arousal and you may best help your child by speaking to his emotional brain. He may be feeling intense and rational thought may not be at its peak. So think about calming the limbic brain in both MOMENTS 2 and 3.

In this specific example, gentle exploration with empathy, caring for the child who has been bitten and modeling calm are the first steps to take. Here is what it may sound like right in the moment, when the biting takes place.

Parent: "Oh, Robert is crying."

"What made him cry?"

"He looks hurt."

"We'd better get an ice pack and a band aide."

"Johnny, please get an ice pack, while I hold Robert with love."

Once the chaos has calmed down, you can circle back for skill building.

"Johnny you seemed mad when Robert got in your space."

"You were afraid he'd take your truck."

"It's okay to be scared, but in our family we do not bite."

"Biting hurts."

"Let's play pretend and practice what you can do instead of biting."

The sample conversation below takes place a few minutes after the crying has stopped and both children are back to wanting to play (MOMENT 3).

Parent: "Johnny, I see that you were really mad."

Johnny: "I want toy!"

Parent: "Yes! You want your toy. Robert took it. You were mad!"

Johnny: "I don't like 'dat!"

Parent: "When you don't like it, say, 'I don't like that! 'Please give it back!' You can ask for help if you need. I will always help you. People are not for biting. You can bite toast and apples. Here, let's practice."

Now, role model what this interaction could like with the desired words and behavior.

When we really think about it, the "Skill Building Opportunity" comes in between MOMENTS 3 and 1. It's like this space of time after you all have calmed down and before another challenge erupts that you practice, role play, plan and prevent. Before another challenge erupts is the "teachable moment", when your child is calm and receptive to new ideas and ways of responding. This is true for every behavioral challenge we can imagine. Capitalize on these moments.

Providing your child the opportunity to practice a better way of handling his anger next time is what skill building is all about. It is far preferable to consequences or punishment.

We know that might not be what you are used to, many of us perceive we need to punish our children when they "misbehave." It's what we've all been taught and what we've all accepted for a long time. We (the authors) are no exception. These concepts were new to us (the authors) at one point in time, also.

We know skill-building is actually constructed within the parent-child interaction, not by sending the child off to his room or to time-out. It makes total sense when you start to use this approach and see a change. Give it a try and notice how things improve. Each time you "practice" using new words or behaviors will build on the last time. This is a process, not an instantaneous cure. While it's tempting, we cannot use this approach a handful of times and decide it's not working. We must stay the course and apply new thoughts, words and behaviors/reactions consistently across time and situations. Think about how many times you had to do multiplication and division drills to help it stick. Brains change and new behaviors are learned over time.

One thing we wish to caution you on is what we call "push back". When you try on this new parenting style, your child may attempt to engage you back into your old "song and dance". They may dig their heels in deeper, intensify their behaviors and give an all-out best effort to derail your attempt at this new approach. In psychology, we call this a "behavioral burst" or "extinction burst". Stars always burn brightest before they burn out. Your child's behavior may intensify as they try to pull you back into your old style of interacting. Resist the pull!

You may want to tell your child, "I know it's hard to get used to this new way of dealing with things. It's hard for all of us. But, I feel good about this new way of talking with you and we will both get used to it."

Now let's reflect on the parent's internal experience. Because how you respond with your facial expressions, body and words will influence whether or not this behavior continues.

"I GOTTA DO SOMETHING QUICK!"

Most of us feel pressure to "do something" when our kids break a family value or social rule. Other parents may even be watching for your response. Such pressure!

The pressure to "do something" generally means we feel pressured to "punish" or to make our child pay for his transgression. Get very clear with what you want for your child. Do you want to have him stop in the immediate future, or do you want to teach him how to do it differently next time? Punishment halts things for the time being, while Bloom Parenting changes behaviors for the long haul.

If you feel you need to do something, do this, The Bloom "Get Calm" Method of empathizing, offering new thoughts, words or actions and practicing new behaviors. The Bloom "Get Calm" Method is designed to move around the defensive brain maintaining a positive connection with your child as you engage the child's "thinker" in collaboration and problem solving. You can apply this process in any situation where you wish to introduce new behavioral strategies to your child.

A key feature of the Bloom Parenting Method is getting out ahead of a persistent challenge by empathizing with your child's feelings and experience before the escalation evolves into an eruption.

We know it may feel like your child goes from 0-60 and perhaps he does. But with planning and practice you can build more time and space between your child's needs and impulses and his intense emotional expression. The way you do this is to empathize before the escalation instead of waiting until the hormones are flowing and the ascent to dysregulation is in full swing.

What follows are three boxes that show you how you use The "Get Calm" Method.

YOU WILL SEE THREE BOXES.

In Box 1: You empathize with your child to help him know you are willing to climb into his shoes with him and figure this out together. Metaphorically, your child hears, "I'm on your side." "I'm in your corner." "How you feel matters to me."

In Box 2: You offer new words, thoughts or actions.

In Box 3: You practice the new words, thoughts or actions with your child.

STEP 1: EMPATHIZE
I see that…
I understand that…
You may be feeling…
It's hard to…

STEP 2: OFFER NEW WORDS OR ACTIONS
I'd like to help you…
I can see this is hard, perhaps we can….
There may be another way to say that, let's find new words …
You might be looking for another way to do that, let's think this out together…
We can do this instead…

STEP 3: PRACTICE
Let's try this…
Let's see what it sounds like…
Let's see what it looks like…

You complete the sentences based on the specific situation. If you feel at a loss for thoughts, words or actions, look at the mantra cards in each chapter. Remember, these sentences are jumping off points. As you become more comfortable collaborating with your child, your ability to revise the sentences will get better and better. You'll want to also keep in mind that the younger the child, the less words you will want to use. It will feel more natural the more you do it.

Where you might have responded, "Stop that right now," "You're in time-out," or "Get with the program," in the past, now you will be responding in a way that engages the child's brain in collaborative problem solving with your child hearing, *"Your experience of this is important to me, together we will find a new way."* That's just part of it, though! You'll also be engaging your child's heart through the use of empathy. **When our heads and hearts are working together, we have a very powerful combination of interventions that bring about enduring change.**

WE TEACH OUR CHILDREN INTO MORE PROSOCIAL-BEHAVIOR

We cannot punish children out of undesirable behavior. We teach them into more pro-social behavior.

In this example, *vinegar, time-outs and biting back*, would teach the lesson that violence leads to more violence. In the long run, these methods can backfire, causing more anger and resentment that lead to more acting out. Assume when your child bites, that he had no other choice available to him at the moment. He needs help finding better alternatives. *The solution is in two parts; managing the physical space between your little ones and giving them words and behavior to express themselves in a new way.*

HOW CAN I TEACH OUR CHILDREN ABOUT PHYSICAL SPACE?

Little kids often walk, crawl and move into each other's space. They reach, grab and intrude. This causes children to feel territorial and often, angry. Managing the space between the children is super helpful.

At one to three years old, your children may need to have space marked off with blue tape, hula-hoops, or other visual signs that say, "This is your space to play."

Next, help your kids find the words for the emotions they're experiencing and encourage them to express them instead of biting. Making statements to your child that communicate, "Hey, I know you are angry," is a good beginning. Then, give your child new words to use. "Please move over." "You are too close to me."

If you see a pattern of biting or acting out, help the children play in their own spaces, until they have the skills to be close without hurting one another. Remain calm to model peaceful play for your children.

HOW DO I CALMLY SET A LIMIT?

Although your intuition tells you to clamp down and be very strict, strive to be counter-intuitive. Become warm and caring, allowing your child to express his emotions. If you yell, he won't learn any new problem-solving skills. If you have a strong emotional reaction to the biting, you may unwittingly encourage more of the biting behavior.

Both children, the 'biter' and the 'bitten,' need your support and attention. It is generally best to provide comfort and assistance to the child who was bitten first. Then, remaining as calm as you can, say to the biter, "Biting hurts people, so it's not allowed." Setting limits for children does not have to be done in anger. A limit is simply the line children are best not to cross. Telling the child clearly and calmly what he can *do instead* helps him replace the old behavior with new, more prosocial behavior.

Many children are used to "hearing a limit" with anger. You may observe a look of surprise on your child's face when you respond calmly and collaboratively the first few times. Your role as a parent is to help your child internalize new skills that will help him behave with caring and compassion not anger and fury. Telling your child what he can do, rather than what he is in trouble for already having done is a new beginning for many parent-child relationships.

Setting limits and boundaries helps your child feel safe enough to practice new skills. So we are not encouraging you to just give in. We are encouraging you to learn how to raise a child who can think better about how he behaves by stepping back, modeling, practicing and offering new ways of being.

WHAT WOULD MODELING LOOK LIKE?

Your empathy towards the child who was bitten will provide effective modeling, leading to new behavior and empathy on your child's part. Your modeling of empathy will enhance your toddler's ability to express caring after he's bitten somebody. Encourage him to assist the injured person by getting them an ice-pack or offering the victim another comfort item.

Parents may ask, "How do I instill empathy in my children?" The best way is to model it by showing compassion for their hurt feelings.

"I GOT BIT!"

To the bitten, if the situation allows, say, "I know it hurts and it's scary to get bitten." Become a detective and discover if and how the bitten child contributed to the incident (by grabbing instead of asking, for instance) so both kids can learn to use their words. Even a one-year-old who grabs his older sibling's toy is capable of starting to learn and understand the meaning of words and actions.

ACT IT OUT TO FIX IT UP.

Role-play the troublesome situations with dolls or trucks. Get down on the floor and work out the problem through play.

You can say, "Looks like the doll took her friend's toy and they both are upset." Being upset is not fun, but they can think about how to work it out." "Maybe they can find two dolls, so they each have one."

NOTICE WHAT IS WORKING.

Noticing when your children are playing well helps. Reward desirable behavior, with a tender touch, comment or hug in order to encourage better choices. Catch your kids doing well and praise it. Be specific, and notice the small stuff. All those little positive behaviors add up to bigger better behaviors over time.

WHAT YOU CAN **SAY**

When we get worried or anxious we want to protect our things.

It's not fun to have our things taken.

When we feel threatened we get angry.

Sometimes we feel angry, when really, we are afraid.

We feel afraid what we like will be taken from us.

We feel afraid we will lose the pleasure we feel in the moment.

When we have strong feelings we can choose to stay calm.

We do not always have to explode or hurt others.

We can turn our feelings down instead of up.

Telling someone 'Please step back,' or 'You are getting in my space,' can help.

Sometimes we need to play in our own spaces.

If we feel ourselves getting angry we need to get some space.

Biting is not how we say we are unhappy. We use our words for that.

Biting hurts other people.

WHAT YOU CAN **THINK**

Biting is a sign my child doesn't have a better way to manage this moment.

My child needs me to help calm his intense emotions.

My child is doing the best he can, right now.

My children need me to teach them how to manage their physical space.

My child isn't intentionally trying to upset his brother.

Children have over-the-top feelings, when they don't have the skills to cope in the moment.

I will stay calm as I show my child a new way to cope instead of biting.

I will give my child the words to use next time.

I will model patience not fury for both our boys.

I feel angry when I feel helpless.

My anger is a sign that I need to problem solve rather than explode.

WHAT YOU CAN **DO**

Describe the relationship between your child's feelings and behavior, "You were mad so you bit."

Empathize with the biter, "Sometimes you get so mad you can't stand it, I get that."

Biting may be the first thing you think of when you are mad. You can choose a cold washcloth to bite instead.

Write it down and draw it out, "Let's draw a picture of what we can do that's safer than biting."

Offer solutions, "Biting may be the first thing you think of, let's choose a cold washcloth to bite, when we are mad."

Show your child how to say he is sorry. "I am sorry I bit you." (We don't recommend forcing a half-hearted "sorry", but do model and encourage it. Eventually kids will do this on their own. Keep modeling and supporting your child.)

Show your child how to help the child who is hurt, "Let's get Robert an ice pack." "We need to help him feel better."

Show your child you are willing to problem solve with him. "It feels bad to hurt someone. We can work on a safer way together."

Role play, when your child is calm, "Let's do this again in a new way."

A FEW LAST WORDS.....

Your child wants to do better, we promise. After the upset, encourage the two kids to restore their relationship by interacting in a fun situation. Children have a remarkable ability to fix hurt feelings by playing. Your children need attention, affection and recognition. Playing on the floor with your child after a tough time provides an opportunity for you to bond while he calms down. We understand that this is a new way of interacting with your child and it will take some getting used to. Simply sitting down and playing something familiar like cars or blocks models for your child that you can remain attached and present, moving on from rough patches, with good self-control and feelings management yourself. Sitting on the floor quietly and engaging in a clear way says to your child, "I can handle this, so can you."

Children learn how to solve problems through play. Ten to fifteen-minutes of floor-play each day can make a world of difference.

Name it, Claim it, Tame it
Helping Kids Deal with Feelings is Easy as 1, 2, 3

NAME IT

Helping kids identify feelings is one of the foundations of self-regulation. Feelings are all around us. Help kids identify feelings in themselves and others. You can do this while reading books, watching a cartoon, or dealing with real life situations. Labeling feelings is an important prerequisite to emotional literacy.

CLAIM IT

When kids can proclaim, "I'm angry!" or "I'm so sad," they take ownership for their feelings. Owning their own feelings provides the springboard for the next step, which is "doing something" proactive about that feeling, rather than acting out because they are ineffective in handling that feeling.

TAME IT

This is the step where your emotion-coaching really kicks in. Helping kids generate healthy, realistic ways to handle feelings of anger and upset is a skill that will contribute to your child's overall success. Ideas might include, "Talk to someone you trust," "Run your anger out," "Draw a picture of what upsets you." These strategies will be even more successful if your child helps identify what might help her. Expressing feelings and making them known to another can be a powerful way to discharge them.

"Shared sorrow is half a sorrow."
~ Swedish Proverb

More tips from Lynne: Three Ways To Get
BrainSmart About Your Child's Biting

SAY

When we get worried or anxious we want to protect our things.

BLOOM 50 Things To Say, Think, And Do With Anxious, Angry, and Over-the-Top Kids

SAY

It's not fun to have our things taken.

BLOOM 50 Things To Say, Think, And Do With Anxious, Angry, and Over-the-Top Kids

SAY

When we feel threatened we get angry.

BLOOM 50 Things To Say, Think, And Do With Anxious, Angry, and Over-the-Top Kids

SAY

Sometimes we feel angry, when really, we are afraid.

BLOOM 50 Things To Say, Think, And Do With Anxious, Angry, and Over-the-Top Kids

SAY

We feel afraid what we like will be taken from us.

BLOOM 50 Things To Say, Think, And Do With Anxious, Angry, and Over-the-Top Kids

SAY

We feel afraid we will lose the pleasure we feel in the moment.

BLOOM 50 Things To Say, Think, And Do With Anxious, Angry, and Over-the-Top Kids

SAY

When we have strong feelings we can choose to stay calm.

SAY

We do not always have to explode or hurt others.

SAY

We can turn our feelings down instead of up.

SAY

Telling someone 'Please step back,' or 'You are getting in my space,' can help.

SAY

Sometimes we need to play in our own spaces.

SAY

If we feel ourselves getting angry we need to get some space.

Biting is not how we say we are unhappy. We use our words for that.

Biting hurts other people.

Biting is a sign my child doesn't have a better way to manage this moment.

My child needs me to help calm his intense emotions.

My child is doing the best he can, right now.

My children need me to teach them how to manage their physical space.

THINK

My child isn't intentionally trying to upset his brother.

THINK

Children have over-the-top feelings, when they don't have the skills to cope in the moment.

THINK

I will stay calm as I show my child a new way to cope instead of biting.

THINK

I will give my child the words to use next time.

THINK

I will model patience not fury for both our boys.

THINK

I feel angry when I feel helpless.

THINK

My anger is a sign that I need to problem solve rather than explode.

BLOOM 50 Things To Say, Think, And Do With Anxious, Angry, and Over-the-Top Kids

DO

Empathize with the biter, "Sometimes you get so mad you can't stand it, I get that."

BLOOM 50 Things To Say, Think, And Do With Anxious, Angry, and Over-the-Top Kids

DO

Describe the relationship between your child's feelings and behavior, "You were mad so you bit."

BLOOM 50 Things To Say, Think, And Do With Anxious, Angry, and Over-the-Top Kids

DO

Offer solutions, "Let's plan for what you can do next time."

BLOOM 50 Things To Say, Think, And Do With Anxious, Angry, and Over-the-Top Kids

DO

Write it down and draw it out, "Let's draw a picture of what we can do that's safer than biting."

BLOOM 50 Things To Say, Think, And Do With Anxious, Angry, and Over-the-Top Kids

DO

Offer solutions, "Biting may be the first thing you think of, let's choose a cold washcloth to bite, when we are mad."

BLOOM 50 Things To Say, Think, And Do With Anxious, Angry, and Over-the-Top Kids

DO

Show your child how to say he is sorry. "I am sorry I bit you."

DO

Show your child how to help the child who is hurt, "Let's get Robert an ice pack." "We need to help him feel better."

DO

Show your child you are willing to problem solve with him. "It feels bad to hurt someone. We can work on a safer way together."

DO

Role play, when your child is calm, "Let's do this again in a new way."

DO

DO

CHAPTER 4

Aggression Alley

HELP FOR HITTING... AND BEYOND

"My four and six-year-old boys are incapable of playing without becoming physical. Sometimes they even escalate to hitting me. Consequences work for the short-term when I initially separate them but the hitting continues when they return to play."

Hitting can be a real frustration for parents. Hitting between siblings upsets everyone. Constant battling disrupts family happiness. Hitting is your children's way of communicating about their feelings and internal sensory experiences. When children resort to hitting, their behavior is telling us that they do not have the tools to solve their problems.

You can imagine that your child is saying to you, 'Hey Mom, my feelings are HUGE and I can't handle them. Here, you hold them for a second and maybe you can manage them better.'" When behaviors escalate it provides us with a golden opportunity to model composure and demonstrate a sense of "being calm under fire".

FEELING TERRITORIAL?

Children hit for many reasons. Most of all, hitting is a form of communicating things are not feeling right. A common reason children hit is because they feel their territory or space has been invaded. Whether at the drinking fountain, playing trains at a toy table, or just sitting in the kitchen eating breakfast, when a young child feels another person in his space, he does not have the words to say, "May I, please, have my physical space back? I am feeling crowded by you, right now." Helping children learn the meaning of physical space, how to define it and how to ask for it back, is a good starting point.

WHEN ARE THE KIDS ALLOWED TO PLAY NEXT TO EACH OTHER?

Talk with the children about using "safe bodies." "In our family, we keep our bodies safe." Using the words, "In our family," builds the family culture. These words are important on many levels. They distinguish your family as a unique entity, one with a certain set of values by which it operates. Give your kids the words to use, "If your body feels like hitting, pushing or shoving, get up and come tell daddy or mommy." "You can play closely together again, when your bodies are being safe." "We need to keep our hands to ourselves and use them for loving not hurting."

"I need my space back." Physical space and body awareness are rarely taught to children. You can show your kids what personal space is by having them hold their elbows up by their sides. Show them that when they play, they are to be an elbow's length apart. Of course, sometimes play is up close. If your child is hitting, they may need your help establishing a safety zone between themselves and their playmate where both can play and not feel intruded upon.

"Let's play the 'Elbows-up game' and show each other how big our personal body space is. Okay, lift up your elbows, now we can all see how much space you each need to play."

LET'S DIG DEEPER

We've chatted a bit about physical space and boundaries, let's consider some other ideas. The reasons for hitting vary for each child, you may wish to consider whether the child is experiencing anger, upset, frustration, disappointment, loneliness or other related emotions. Few children hit when they are happy. Hitting is a way of saying, "This really is not working for me right now." "My feelings are TOO BIG." "I do not have the skills to work this out in a more cooperative way." A child who is hitting is asking you to help them!

Our children hit to express themselves and get their needs met. If they had another way to manage their feelings and relationships, they would do so. Most children and adults do the best they can, in the moment, with the skills they have. That is why it is so helpful to watch for the signs that hitting may be coming.

IN A NUTSHELL: WHAT MAKES CHILDREN HIT?

- Many children hit to express their feelings of anger, disappointment, frustration, and sadness. If they had the words to get their needs met without hitting, they likely would use them.

- Some children feel territorial about their space and do not have the words to say, "Can you please back up, you are in my personal space."

- Over-crowding and sensory over-stimulation can cause children to hit. They feel encroached upon and they hit in an effort to obtain more physical space.

- Children, especially those close in age, can feel territorial or jealous. A sibling may be dominating them or they may feel ignored, left-out or lonely.

- Some children hit to gain control in the social hierarchy.

- Children hit to get something they want (a toy, a position in line, etc.).

- Parents can put their kids over the edge by bombarding them with words, directions and instructions. Ask yourself, "Do I use too many words?"

- Children may be the emotional barometers in the family. When things are going wrong, often the children notice first. Their behavior is just an outward manifestation of something that is amiss within the family unit.

HOW CAN I READ MY CHILD'S SUBTLE CUES?

Children may not have the cognitive ability, vocabulary, or insight to recognize that the above things are what come into play prior to hitting. When you are aware of the subtle social contexts and cues that can lead to hitting, you are much better able to assist your child in moving through this behavior.

It's important to note that hitting is not necessarily a maladaptive behavior in young children, albeit socially unacceptable. We must be careful not to assign adult motives to young children. "He's aggressive." "She's mean." Young children are just learning about relational interactions and hitting is a sign that you need to step up the support you give, to help your child through this phase.

Observing your child's body language, space and words helps you provide your child with alternate behaviors before the hitting occurs. If the hitting has already happened, your child may be too angry or frustrated to problem solve with you. In this case, it is preferable to go back later to role-playing and modeling for the child, possible words and actions he could use to choose a behavior other than hitting.

CAN YOU PLEASE LEND ME YOUR BRAIN?

If you have a child who flies off the handle easily, remember that you need to be the child's brain. A young child's prefrontal cortex is far from developed. This means it is challenging for him to "think" about a socially acceptable alternative to get the computer, the shirt they want to wear (it's in the laundry), or the cherished toy.

In essence, your child is "hijacked" by his emotional brain. He wants what he wants when he wants it. He resorts to being physical as the quickest path to getting his needs met. That is where parenting and teaching comes in. It's our job to help be the child's brain until they are more mature, and can choose more socially appropriate behaviors. In essence, we are loaning our child our prefrontal cortexes, or highest thinking part of our brains. In so doing, we help them learn problem-solving skills while modeling a calm, relaxed state.

This exchange is called co-regulation. You are literally helping your child calm down. Eventually, co-regulation will give way to self-regulation, where your child will be able to calm down on his own.

> The success of our child's ability to self-regulate later in life is related to their experience of clear, consistent, and responsive mutual regulation in the early years. It's an amazing, delicate dance that parents and children engage in.

This is why keeping ourselves calm is so important. We should make every effort to calm our own limbic (emotional) brains, so that we can show our kids just how to do it. If you grew up with parents who couldn't (for whatever reason) manage their own emotional reactions, and you struggle with it in your life, reach out to a qualified and licensed mental health professional. You will be amazed at the difference this makes in the quality of your life and the lives of your children. Everyone benefits with solid self-regulation.

If I don't understand Latin, I would be very hard pressed to help my child study for a Latin test. It's the same with emotional literacy. If I'm not sure how to calm myself down, I'll have a much more difficult time teaching my child how to do so. Luckily, help can be found in the context of counseling or therapy. Seeking out such help is a strength, not a weakness.

WHAT YOU CAN **SAY**

We often want things we cannot have.

Waiting is one of the hardest things to do.

Can we find the words to say, "May I please have that back?"

If your body wants to hit or push, it's time to choose a new solution.

You don't like it when someone has the toy you want to play with.

I see your body is tense, maybe you feel frustrated, afraid or angry.

Maybe, you can cross your arms in front of your body or put your hands in your pockets to keep yourself from hitting.

What are some things we can do with our hands to keep them from hitting?

Maybe, you can fill your hands by holding your blanket or your stuffed animal.

If you feel like hitting, take a step back and go ask an adult for help.

Let's make a list of other things we can do like breathe, ask your teacher for help, or tell the other child, Please walk away I am busy.

Anger and fear are BIG feelings, but I can help you learn to handle them!

Your anger feels really heavy right now, how about if I hold if for a while?

Nobody likes to be told 'no', but we can learn to accept it, even if we don't like it.

I can help you manage your feelings by talking about them with you.

WHAT YOU CAN **THINK**

In our family we can experience a range of feelings, what we do with those feelings is what counts.

My child is simply saying, "I need your help."

I am going to manage this head-on. All of my child's feelings are okay. My job is to help him manage them.

The skills I teach my child, will make me a better person as well.

I am going to remain calm and show my child that he can stay calm as well.

I am going to think about my own response before I take action.

How I respond will determine the skills my child learns over time.

Together, my child and I will work this out.

One moment at a time, my child will develop better coping skills.

I am doing my very best and growing as a parent every day.

WHAT YOU CAN **DO**

Empathize with your child's experience. "I can see that this is really hard for you."

Focus on the good, "I see you thinking about what you do with your hands more now that we talked about how hitting hurts."

Help your child see himself as thoughtful, "You are kind and thoughtful."

Validating your children's feelings is the best way to teach kids to be caring as they grow.

Remember validation is saying, "I hear you and I understand you." You can understand your child's behavior without agreeing that it's okay.

Provide hope by sending the message, hard feelings get easier to manage as you learn new skills.

Model for your child how to say, "I'm sorry."

"I'm Sorry" *(two little words that make a big difference.)* We do not believe in forcing a young child to say he is sorry. We do, however, believe in modeling it and encouraging it. "I'm sorry" makes everyone feel better.

IN CLOSING...

It can be frustrating for parents when children hit their sibling, or worse, when you get that call from the school. As parents we feel embarrassed, overwhelmed and sometimes angry ourselves. Planning, practicing, and role-playing better solutions when your children are calm, arms them with more effective tools when the going gets rough. As a child, it is aggravating to be denied what you want. If they do not have the cognitive and emotional skills to remain calm and think things through, they act out. Providing guidance through these tricky social interactions is a much quicker path to socially acceptable behaviors than punishment and shaming could ever be.

> The key is to have a loving parent or teacher who provides you with new words and behaviors to help you become a more successful social being. Kids who are given this advantage, rather than having punishment meted out, receive a rare gift, they in turn share with others throughout their lives.

More tips from Lynne: Four Expert Ways
to Curb Aggressive Behavior in Children

SAY

We often want things we cannot have.

BLOOM 50 Things To Say, Think, And Do With Anxious, Angry, and Over-the-Top Kids

SAY

Waiting is one of the hardest things to do.

BLOOM 50 Things To Say, Think, And Do With Anxious, Angry, and Over-the-Top Kids

SAY

Can we find the words to say, 'May I please have that back?'

BLOOM 50 Things To Say, Think, And Do With Anxious, Angry, and Over-the-Top Kids

SAY

If your body wants to hit or push, it's time to choose a new solution.

BLOOM 50 Things To Say, Think, And Do With Anxious, Angry, and Over-the-Top Kids

SAY

You don't like it when someone has the toy you want to play with.

BLOOM 50 Things To Say, Think, And Do With Anxious, Angry, and Over-the-Top Kids

SAY

I see your body is tense, maybe you feel frustrated, afraid or angry.

BLOOM 50 Things To Say, Think, And Do With Anxious, Angry, and Over-the-Top Kids

SAY

Maybe, you can cross your arms in front of your body or put your hands in your pockets to keep yourself from hitting.

SAY

What are some things we can do with our hands to keep them from hitting?

SAY

Maybe, you can fill your hands by holding your blanket or your stuffed animal.

SAY

If you feel like hitting, take a step back and go ask an adult for help.

SAY

Let's make a list of other things we can do like breathe, ask your teacher for help, or tell the other child, Please walk away I am busy.

SAY

Anger and fear are BIG feelings, but I can help you learn to handle them!

SAY

Your anger feels really heavy right now, how about if I hold if for a while?

SAY

Nobody likes to be told 'no', but we can learn to accept it, even if we don't like it.

SAY

I can help you manage your feelings by talking about them with you.

SAY

SAY

SAY

THINK

In our family we can experience a range of feelings, what we do with those feelings is what counts.

BLOOM 50 Things To Say, Think, And Do With Anxious, Angry, and Over-the-Top Kids

THINK

I am going to manage this head-on. All of my child's feelings are okay. My job is to help him manage them.

BLOOM 50 Things To Say, Think, And Do With Anxious, Angry, and Over-the-Top Kids

THINK

How I respond will determine the skills my child learns over time.

BLOOM 50 Things To Say, Think, And Do With Anxious, Angry, and Over-the-Top Kids

THINK

My child is simply saying, "I need your help."

BLOOM 50 Things To Say, Think, And Do With Anxious, Angry, and Over-the-Top Kids

THINK

One moment at a time, my child will develop better coping skills.

BLOOM 50 Things To Say, Think, And Do With Anxious, Angry, and Over-the-Top Kids

THINK

Together, my child and I will work this out.

BLOOM 50 Things To Say, Think, And Do With Anxious, Angry, and Over-the-Top Kids

THINK

I am doing my
very best
and growing
as a parent
every day.

BLOOM 50 Things To Say, Think, And Do With Anxious, Angry, and Over-the-Top Kids

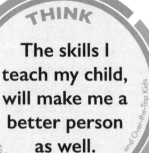

THINK

The skills I
teach my child,
will make me a
better person
as well.

BLOOM 50 Things To Say, Think, And Do With Anxious, Angry, and Over-the-Top Kids

THINK

I am going to
remain calm and
show my child
that he can stay
calm as well.

BLOOM 50 Things To Say, Think, And Do With Anxious, Angry, and Over-the-Top Kids

THINK

I am going to
think about my
own response
before I take
action.

BLOOM 50 Things To Say, Think, And Do With Anxious, Angry, and Over-the-Top Kids

THINK

BLOOM 50 Things To Say, Think, And Do With Anxious, Angry, and Over-the-Top Kids

THINK

BLOOM 50 Things To Say, Think, And Do With Anxious, Angry, and Over-the-Top Kids

DO

Focus on the good, "I see you thinking about what you do with your hands more now that we talked about how hitting hurts."

BLOOM 50 Things To Say, Think, And Do With Anxious, Angry, and Over-the-Top Kids

DO

Help your child see himself as thoughtful, "You are kind and thoughtful."

BLOOM 50 Things To Say, Think, And Do With Anxious, Angry, and Over-the-Top Kids

DO

Empathize with your child's experience. "I can see that this is really hard for you."

BLOOM 50 Things To Say, Think, And Do With Anxious, Angry, and Over-the-Top Kids

DO

Validating your children's feelings is the best way to teach kids to be caring as they grow.

BLOOM 50 Things To Say, Think, And Do With Anxious, Angry, and Over-the-Top Kids

DO

Remember validation is saying, "I hear you and I understand you." You can understand your child's behavior without agreeing that it's okay.

BLOOM 50 Things To Say, Think, And Do With Anxious, Angry, and Over-the-Top Kids

DO

Provide hope by sending the message, hard feelings get easier to manage as you learn new skills. Model for your child how to say, "I'm sorry."

BLOOM 50 Things To Say, Think, And Do With Anxious, Angry, and Over-the-Top Kids

CHAPTER 5

Daunting Disrespect

THE SASS IS THE SAUCE

"When my six-year-old does not get her way she is sassy, disrespectful and rude. She appears entitled and unmanageable. What makes her act this way and how do I change her behavior?"

WHAT IS THE SASSING ALL ABOUT?

Sassing is disrespectful back talk. Usually sassing is about feeling lost, alone and unlikable. We know these kids seem so self-assured but really they can feel poorly about themselves, or perhaps powerless. Sassing can also be about loss of respect or a sense of emotional intrusion. In your family, make "being respectful" a primary value that is spoken about and modeled by parents and children alike.

WHAT CAN I DO TO MINIMIZE THE SASS?

Non-verbal communication is more powerful than words, so keep your eye on your own non-verbal language. Many parents are unaware they use eye-rolling and frustrated faces as a way of communicating. This can contribute to the escalation between parent and child. We cannot expect our children to choose behaviors we do not model ourselves as parents. They may also imitate the behavior of other family members.

CAN OUR FAMILY SITUATION BE PART OF THE PROBLEM?

Sassing can be a way your child communicates that her sensory system is on overload. Imagine your child is saying, "I cannot hear you, understand you, or respond politely because you yell too much, speak too loudly and listen too little."

Sassing can also be about overwhelming siblings. Does your younger child have an older sibling who is hiding behind online gaming or screaming out with poor behavior? Can you hear your child saying inside, "I am so tired of my older sister bossing both you and me around. This whole family feels out-of-control."

WHAT IS THE SASSING REALLY SAYING?

Sassing can be a way of communicating, "My emotional needs are not being met." "I'm overwhelmed." "I'm being disrespected." "You are not hearing me so I create an attitude." "I don't know what to do with my feelings." "You guys are emotionally not there." "You let my older brother run the show." "What the heck, you expect me to be polite when you guys are downright mean to one another." "When you start being polite and respectful as parents, I'll do the same." **Wow!** **What if that was what your child was trying to say to you?**

Kids who resort to being sassy may be feeling sad, unhappy, powerless, left-out, lonely, misunderstood, irritated, frustrated or angry.

IS MY CHILD JUST BEING MANIPULATIVE?

Rather than thinking of your child as being manipulative or rude, imagine that she is trying to communicate with you, yet lacks the words. What comes out as sass may be more a reflection of your child not having the vocabulary or the emotional insight to say, "I'm frustrated and overwhelmed. This is really hard for me right now. I just don't know what to do." Instead, you hear, "Whatever, I'm not listening to you," or even, "I hate you!" Before you send your child packing to her room, or the nearest corner, know that particular strategy is not going to make things better in the future. If you want to help your child build a skill, you have to slow down and think really carefully about what she needs. She often doesn't know herself. If she did, the two of you wouldn't be stuck in this interaction.

When children sass, it may also be their last ditch effort to get their way. It may be their way to vie for more power in the parent-child relationship. When people, including kids, feel powerless, they may resort to any number of negative behaviors. Just think of the ways in which adults sometimes act when they don't get their way, when others don't agree with them, or they feel they are getting the short end of the stick.

WHY SASSING IS SUCH A CHALLENGE

We know sassing is really a challenge for adults and educators. The child's defensive brain is engaging our defensive brain, and when that happens, all bets are off. We can put a halt to this back-and-forth negative interaction, by better understanding the historical and subjective context of it all.

Historically, societal expectations have dictated that children be respectful in all circumstances. We *all* like respectful children. We all aim to raise kids who consistently demonstrate good moral character. We view anything less as flagrant and belligerent disregard to social conventions. We might even project our child 20 or 30 years into the future, imagining them with failed relationships, being fired from a job, and worse. Those things could well happen, if your child didn't have your love and guidance. There are lots of years for teaching and modeling before it comes to that. Quite simply, this sort of behavior is proof that your child needs your guidance.

Subjectively, we tend to personalize those quarrelsome rants and accept them at face value, rather than digging deeper. Our own limbic systems are firing and we are reduced to the fight/flight response ourselves. We swing into protective mode and our first reaction may be to punish. However, if you find yourself having to dole out consequences to a child on a regular basis for disrespect, it becomes clear that the consequences do little to change the behavior.

Attuning to your child, recognizing the emotional hurts underneath the venomous outburst, allowing the child's limbic system to reset and processing the upset beneath the words, provides a much quicker route to a child who can learn how to process and digest BIG feelings. This takes a change on our part, first. We have to unlearn our old ways of doing things and it isn't easy.

There is perhaps no other circumstance in parenting, teaching or caring for children that calls upon us to self-regulate more than when we are dealing with disrespectful, sassy children. We often recognize this as a direct attack, an assault to all of our senses, and our intuitive response is one of fighting back. We know, because we've experienced it, too. However, Bloom Parenting helps us understand the cause of this behavior in a cognitive, emotional and visceral way, so we can help our kids move forward much more quickly. Bloom Parenting provides us with insight to the inner workings of our child's heart and mind.

> Calm = effective. It's useful to ask yourself, "Is my goal to control my child or to teach her how to control herself?"

The key is to create an emotionally and physically safe home in which the family culture is kindness. Once this is the trusted norm, you simply respond to your child, "In our family we speak kindly." "In our family we use a caring tone." "I'm hearing that your tone is disrespectful. Please try again." If you are consistent and your family models polite language, your child will eventually comply. This takes time and effort. Stay the course!

HOW LONG WILL THIS TAKE? I NEED MY CHILD TO STOP SASSING NOW!

Change is not an overnight phenomenon. Experts note that it takes time for our habits to begin to change. That means you need to provide intentional and ongoing support for your child to help her align with the family values you are trying to teach. Each time you provide more guidance or coach your child emotionally, you are building new pathways in her brain to replace the older, unwanted behaviors. Do you notice how we are not only asking our children to change, but we are changing right alongside them? Our own resistance or hesitation to this illustrates just how hard these kinds of changes can be. Be gentle with your child and yourself.

If your child does not adopt a new tone, continue to look at your own behavior. You may be missing how your communication is rude, unkind, disrespectful, condescending or sarcastic. We cannot expect our children to use kind non-verbal gestures and a loving tone, if they do not see respect modeled in everyday life. This can be really tough for both parents and kids, but the rewards make it so worthwhile.

DO YOU HEAR WHAT I HEAR?

Sometimes kids who sass hear adults speak poorly of others (on the phone or in the car), talk behind people's backs, or use a derogatory tone themselves. Play detective and keep an eye on your own behavior.

Kids who sass may have an older sibling, friend or adult role model, who demonstrates disrespect. Think about whom in the family that might be. Children copy what we do, not what we tell them to do.

WHAT YOU CAN **SAY**

I can hear that you want something but your tone is in the way of my understanding exactly what it is.

Do you want to try to tell me again what you want?

I can hear by your words that you are feeling stressed!

It looks like you're feeling _____ (angry, frustrated, irritated, upset, hurt).

It's okay to be mad, but it's not okay to be sarcastic.

Drawing out your feelings or telling a story about how you want things to be different helps solve problems.

If your body feels so angry, let's figure out why.

People listen to you better when you talk in a calm voice and use kind words. Here, let's practice how that might sound.

Do you need help figuring out how to say it differently?

Having those feelings is okay, but in our house, we talk with each other respectfully.

It's okay to have many different feelings. It's what we choose to do with our feelings that matters.

When you talk like that, it tells me you're not very happy inside.

When you use mean, fighting words, it tells me you have some big feelings that are bothering you. Let's talk about those feelings.

Is there part of you that thinks other people in our family are sassy, rude or impolite, as well?

Help me understand what you see or hear in our family that tells you that you can be rude or impolite.

I'm confused. Who is using a mean, rude or sarcastic tone with you? Let's talk about that.

When you speak with your teacher today, remember to use a kind tone, a quiet voice and a soft body.

Do your best! I know you can do it!

WHAT YOU CAN **THINK**

Think feelings first when talking with sassy kids, because "the sass" is like "the sauce," hiding all the feelings.

Remember, "You can be right or you can be in a relationship." Being in a relationship means that you do not need to assert power and control.

Calm = effective. It's useful to ask yourself, "Is my goal to control my child or to teach her how to control herself?"

The way my child holds her body tells me she may be more angry than she knows.

My child is crying out for help.

My child seems in control, but she feels small and insecure.

I'm going to consider my role in all this, what's my part?

I'm going to make sure I am being respectful with my words, tone and body.

I am going to put in the emotional effort to really connect with my child and better understand what's going on inside their mind.

I'm going to set limits with love not anger.

I'm going to focus my words and actions on the goal of raising a child who respects herself more. Sassing says she doesn't like herself very much.

When my child sasses, it's a sign she isn't able to process her overwhelming feelings.

I can take this sassing as a sign that my child needs more guidance and support around handling feelings of anger and upset.

WHAT YOU CAN **DO**

Sometimes under the sass is a child who needs to cry. When you redirect the sass, you may get a lot of tears. Just be there to listen.

Ask your child if she has another way to make the request. If not, offer her a new sentence using a polite tone, so that she can model after you.

If your child continues sassing, stay neutral. Simply say, "I'll be able to hear what you need when you're speaking in a calm, respectful voice, like I am."

Be calm even when your child is talking to you in an infuriating tone. If you meet anger with anger, you both lose. This is difficult, but you'll get better at it the more you practice. Imagine being a customer service specialist dealing with an unsatisfied customer. You would hear them out, stay calm and look for a solution. You might process your feelings about it with a co-worker or supervisor, later. As a parent, you can share with a friend or partner how frustrated you really were when dealing with your child. Keeping a "customer service" approach, polite and willing to help, when kids are really struggling, can work wonders!

Lower your voice, whisper or move more slowly. This tells the defensive brain (the limbic system), I am not in fight mode, so you have the space to calm down and be heard. The calmer you are, the more effective you will be.

Breathe, resist sarcasm, contempt and devaluation yourself. These are relationship breakers.

Collaboratively role-play conversing in a variety of voices with your child, so that she can hear the difference. Sad, mad, sarcastic, disappointed, angry, critical... In fact, we recommend practicing role-playing how a person might look or sound when they have a variety of feelings. This helps increase your child's emotional literacy and improves their ability to identify their feelings as well as the feelings of others. Do this when your child is calm and well-rested for maximum benefit.

Make a list of five family calming strategies and put them on the fridge for easy access.

You need to give your child new words, verbal tone and body language that say, "I want to learn with you," not "I want to dominate you."

When your child is at their peak of sassiness, it's okay to disengage. This does not mean emotionally or physically abandoning your child. Tell her, "I'm going to give you some space to calm down. I'd love to talk to you when you are relaxed." If she appears ready to collaborate you can offer to do a calming skill with her: "Would you like us to do some deep breathing together to calm down?" If she's just on fire, give her some space and do the same for yourself. It's crucial that you stay calm and kind when you say this. If your tone sounds demeaning or sarcastic you'll both lose. Circle back later for the teaching, not while she is 'locked and loaded'.

> In a moment of stress we can: Close our eyes and imagine a beautiful beach. Sit on the floor and breathe deeply ten times. Walk outside and experience the fresh air. Sit in a comfy chair and read a book. Put our heads down on a pillow and listen to enjoyable music.
>
> As parents, we cannot always control our child's tone, words or behavior, but we can always control our responses.

IN A NUTSHELL: WHAT MAKES CHILDREN SASSY?

Children may be expressing frustration, anxiety, anger, disappointment, or even embarrassment. They have not yet learned how to process these feelings and need your guidance.

Children may be trying to regain control when they feel they are losing the battle.

In some families, the parental hierarchy is out-of-order and the children try to gain the upper-hand and assert themselves as "in-charge".

Perhaps in the past, sassing got them what they wanted.

Some children feel ignored. They would rather have negative attention than no attention at all.

There are times when children do not feel they are "being understood" by adults.

When adults roll their eyes or speak in a disrespectful way to family members and friends, the children may copy it.

Kids do what they see, not what they are told to do. Do you (or the older siblings, extended family members) use a negative tone? Are you yelling or demeaning when you speak with your children, spouse/partner, or on the phone with customer service people? Our children watch and learn from our every move.

> The calmer you are, the more effective you will be.

IN CLOSING...

Our actions show our children how to behave. Even while under duress, we teach them how to express their emotions appropriately. Then they feel much more comfortable saying, "I'm mad at you. I want to buy a new skirt and you won't let me," instead of sticking out their tongues and inciting our fury. As long as your child expresses her feelings without sarcasm or contempt, allow her the space to have these feelings without getting angry with her. This is preferable to hearing, "I hate you!" "You're not a good mom!" "You never let me do anything!"

Sassy kids can look pretty powerful to an outsider, like your neighbor or even the school teacher. Sassy kids like to throw their weight around. But inside they are hurting. Sassy kids don't like themselves very much, they do not feel loved at the moment and they don't feel competent. Helping your sassy child learn the boundaries and expectations in your family culture and modeling respectful communication will essentially "set her free" from her negative view of herself.

More tips from Wendy: Three Things You Should Never Do if You Want Your Child to Stop Sassing

SAY

I can hear that you want something but your tone is in the way of my understanding exactly what it is.

BLOOM 50 Things To Say, Think, And Do With Anxious, Angry, and Over-the-Top Kids

SAY

Do you want to try to tell me again what you want?

BLOOM 50 Things To Say, Think, And Do With Anxious, Angry, and Over-the-Top Kids

SAY

I can hear by your words that you are feeling stressed!

BLOOM 50 Things To Say, Think, And Do With Anxious, Angry, and Over-the-Top Kids

SAY

It looks like you're feeling

_____

(angry, frustrated, irritated, upset, hurt).

BLOOM 50 Things To Say, Think, And Do With Anxious, Angry, and Over-the-Top Kids

SAY

It's okay to be mad, but it's not okay to be sarcastic.

BLOOM 50 Things To Say, Think, And Do With Anxious, Angry, and Over-the-Top Kids

SAY

Drawing out your feelings or telling a story about how you want things to be different helps solve problems.

BLOOM 50 Things To Say, Think, And Do With Anxious, Angry, and Over-the-Top Kids

SAY

If your body feels so angry, let's figure out why.

BLOOM 50 Things To Say, Think, And Do With Anxious, Angry, and Over-the-Top Kids

SAY

People listen to you better when you talk in a calm voice and use kind words. Here, let's practice how that might sound.

BLOOM 50 Things To Say, Think, And Do With Anxious, Angry, and Over-the-Top Kids

SAY

Do you need help figuring out how to say it differently?

BLOOM 50 Things To Say, Think, And Do With Anxious, Angry, and Over-the-Top Kids

SAY

Having those feelings is okay, but in our house, we talk with each other respectfully.

BLOOM 50 Things To Say, Think, And Do With Anxious, Angry, and Over-the-Top Kids

SAY

It's okay to have many different feelings. It's what we choose to do with our feelings that matters.

BLOOM 50 Things To Say, Think, And Do With Anxious, Angry, and Over-the-Top Kids

SAY

When you talk like that, it tells me you're not very happy inside.

BLOOM 50 Things To Say, Think, And Do With Anxious, Angry, and Over-the-Top Kids

SAY

When you use mean, fighting words, it tells me you have some big feelings that are bothering you. Let's talk about those feelings.

BLOOM 50 Things To Say, Think, And Do With Anxious, Angry, and Over-the-Top Kids

SAY

Is there part of you that thinks other people in our family are sassy, rude or impolite, as well?

BLOOM 50 Things To Say, Think, And Do With Anxious, Angry, and Over-the-Top Kids

SAY

Help me understand what you see or hear in our family that tells you that you can be rude or impolite.

BLOOM 50 Things To Say, Think, And Do With Anxious, Angry, and Over-the-Top Kids

SAY

I'm confused. Who is using a mean, rude or sarcastic tone with you? Let's talk about that.

BLOOM 50 Things To Say, Think, And Do With Anxious, Angry, and Over-the-Top Kids

SAY

When you speak with your teacher today, remember to use a kind tone, a quiet voice and a soft body. Do your best! I know you can do it!

BLOOM 50 Things To Say, Think, And Do With Anxious, Angry, and Over-the-Top Kids

SAY

BLOOM 50 Things To Say, Think, And Do With Anxious, Angry, and Over-the-Top Kids

THINK

My child seems in control, but she feels small and insecure.

THINK

I'm going to consider my role in all this, what's my part?

THINK

I'm going to make sure I am being respectful with my words, tone and body.

THINK

I am going to put in the emotional effort to really connect with my child and better understand what's going on inside their mind.

THINK

I'm going to set limits with love not anger.

THINK

I'm going to focus my words and actions on the goal of raising a child who respects herself more. Sassing says she doesn't like herself very much.

THINK

Think feelings first when talking with sassy kids, because "the sass" is like "the sauce," hiding all the feelings.

BLOOM 50 Things To Say, Think, And Do With Anxious, Angry, and Over-the-Top Kids

THINK

Remember, "You can be right or you can be in a relationship."

BLOOM 50 Things To Say, Think, And Do With Anxious, Angry, and Over-the-Top Kids

THINK

Being in a relationship means that you do not need to assert power and control.

BLOOM 50 Things To Say, Think, And Do With Anxious, Angry, and Over-the-Top Kids

THINK

Calm = effective. It's useful to ask yourself, "Is my goal to control my child or to teach her how to control herself?"

BLOOM 50 Things To Say, Think, And Do With Anxious, Angry, and Over-the-Top Kids

THINK

The way my child holds her body tells me she may be more angry than she knows. My child is crying out for help.

BLOOM 50 Things To Say, Think, And Do With Anxious, Angry, and Over-the-Top Kids

THINK

When my child sasses, it's a sign she isn't able to process her overwhelming feelings.

BLOOM 50 Things To Say, Think, And Do With Anxious, Angry, and Over-the-Top Kids

DO

Ask your child if she has another way to make the request. If not, offer her a new sentence using a polite tone, so that she can model after you.

BLOOM 50 Things To Say, Think, And Do With Anxious, Angry, and Over-the-Top Kids

DO

Sometimes under the sass is a child who needs to cry. When you redirect the sass, you may get a lot of tears. Just be there to listen.

BLOOM 50 Things To Say, Think, And Do With Anxious, Angry, and Over-the-Top Kids

DO

If your child continues sassing, stay neutral. Simply say, "I'll be able to hear what you need when you're speaking in a calm, respectful voice, like I am."

BLOOM 50 Things To Say, Think, And Do With Anxious, Angry, and Over-the-Top Kids

DO

Be calm even when your child is talking to you in an infuriating tone. If you meet anger with anger, you both lose. This is difficult, but you'll get better at it the more you practice.

BLOOM 50 Things To Say, Think, And Do With Anxious, Angry, and Over-the-Top Kids

DO

Lower your voice, whisper or move more slowly. This tells the defensive brain, I am not in fight mode, so you have the space to calm down and be heard. The calmer you are, the more effective you will be.

BLOOM 50 Things To Say, Think, And Do With Anxious, Angry, and Over-the-Top Kids

DO

Breathe, resist sarcasm, contempt and devaluation yourself. These are relationship breakers.

BLOOM 50 Things To Say, Think, And Do With Anxious, Angry, and Over-the-Top Kids

DO

Collaboratively role-play conversing in a variety of voices with your child, so that she can hear the difference. Sad, mad, sarcastic, disappointed, angry, critical...

BLOOM 50 Things To Say, Think, And Do With Anxious, Angry, and Over-the-Top Kids

DO

Make a list of five family calming strategies and put them on the fridge for easy access.

BLOOM 50 Things To Say, Think, And Do With Anxious, Angry, and Over-the-Top Kids

DO

In a moment of stress we can: Close our eyes and imagine a beautiful beach. Sit on the floor and breathe deeply ten times. Walk outside and experience the fresh air. Sit in a comfy chair and read a book. Put our heads down on a pillow and listen to enjoyable music.

BLOOM 50 Things To Say, Think, And Do With Anxious, Angry, and Over-the-Top Kids

DO

As parents, we cannot always control our child's tone, words or behavior, but we can always control our responses.

BLOOM 50 Things To Say, Think, And Do With Anxious, Angry, and Over-the-Top Kids

DO

You need to give your child new words, verbal tone and body language that say, "I want to learn with you," not "I want to dominate you."

BLOOM 50 Things To Say, Think, And Do With Anxious, Angry, and Over-the-Top Kids

DO

When your child is at their peak of sassiness, it's okay to disengage. This does not mean emotionally or physically abandoning your child. Tell her, "I'm going to give you some space to calm down."

BLOOM 50 Things To Say, Think, And Do With Anxious, Angry, and Over-the-Top Kids

CHAPTER 6

Tell, Don't Yell

CALMING THE CHAOS

"The yelling is out-of-control. My kid is over-the-top-with intensity. He shouts out strings of expletives that make us cringe. My husband and I know we are part of this equation. While we see what we do, we don't know how to change it."

HOW DID IT COME TO THIS?

We have never met a parent who meant to be in this place. We all imagine warm, meaningful relationships with our children. But it can be hard to translate that into action. It's impressive that you take ownership of your contribution to the problem. In simple terms, your yelling became part of your family code. This in turn may have contributed to your child's intensity. It's also true that some children are born with temperamental intensities. When a child like this also lives in a home with yelling, it can be a double whammy. Without laying blame, now you're asking, "How can we calm down, so he can calm down?"

WHAT'S BEHIND THESE EXPLOSIONS?

It's a question we often get from parents and teachers. We offer you this...

It could be that your child is feeling frustrated or angry, and that he has learned this is what one does to make the announcement, "I've reached my limit!" When we bear in mind that emotion is energy in motion, it makes sense that a child's frustration will come out in some manner. When a child has not been taught to express frustration or anger appropriately, his feelings may be expressed in a variety of undesirable ways. Both you and your child will feel better when everyone's mood management is better. Getting and staying calm is a skill that can be learned. Punishment and consequences do little to help this child learn healthier alternatives. Teaching him new skills and a better way to express his feelings is the best answer.

> Emotions are energy in motion. They can be expressed in adaptive or maladaptive ways. Teach your children energy management for a better tomorrow.

WHAT'S THE BRAIN GOT TO DO WITH IT?

The kind of behavioral outburst mentioned is another example of being 'held hostage' in one's emotional brain. A child reaches the point of no return where his emotions are concerned and simply lacks an acceptable way to express that intense feeling. Often, he cannot make a socially appropriate response because he does not know one. Even if he does know a better way (i.e., has been taught one), his abilities may not be up to the task. Once your child reaches the emotional tipping point, he cannot access the higher, thinking part of his brain. Our interactive goals are to be BrainSmart and HeartSmart by moving around our child's defensive brain and appealing to his positive emotions. Learning new emotional skills takes time, practice and support from a calm, emotionally present parent. Only in this manner will new pathways in the brain develop and become a more natural way of responding. This takes time and repetition, so be committed for the long haul.

I'VE SEEN OTHER KIDS GET UPSET, BUT MY CHILD SEEMS TO DO IT ALL THE TIME. IS THIS NORMAL?

Emotions can be tough to handle. This is especially true for young children who have less life experience from which to draw and fewer coping skills in their tool boxes. They can become disappointed, frustrated and irate. They need you to show them how to manage it all.

Sometimes, temperament is at play. Some kids come into this world and are hard-wired to have strong reactions to certain experiences. They may have sensory processing challenges or just experience life in an over-the-top manner. If intensity is an issue, you may see extreme responses to seemingly insignificant situations. Some children (or adults) seem to 'lose it' consistently and leave folks around them feeling perplexed and overwhelmed. All kids (and adults) can learn to manage their intensities, though it may take a bit longer to master. Helping your child identify when he feels intense, what that feels like, where he feels it and how to appropriately discharge or metabolize that energy is key.

Having activities ready-at-hand to offer your child in the intense moment can help. "Do we need to let your energy out it to calm it down?" "If we want to let your energy out we can go kick the soccer ball or even run up and down the sidewalk." "If we want to calm your energy down we can meditate to music for a moment, do a few yoga positions or even simply lie on the floor and let our energy melt into the floor." Allow your creative ideas to flow, stick with it, stay patient and believe that change can happen.

SOMETIMES ANGER IS HURT FEELINGS

With a touch of exploration and communication, you turn a confusing situation into a teachable moment. You can show how hurt feelings build up over time and explode. Little slights that seemingly go unnoticed can add up to create mountains of anger or pain. Next time a family member explodes, see if you can figure out (even draw or write out) all the little hurts and disappointments that built up over the week that led to the outburst. Of course, as always, you'll need to make sure everyone has calmed down and is able to process and think about all the little things that added up to contribute to the explosion. It's a very worthwhile endeavor and one we highly recommend.

THE LITTLE HURTS BETWEEN JOHNNY AND MOMMY

Eleven-year-old Johnny was so excited to see his mom return home from work every evening. Night after night he would run up to her with his basketball, "I can shoot hoops, Mom wanna see?" His mother, worn-out from another tough day at work would respond, "Tonight I'm tired, maybe tomorrow." Then she would sit down to watch television with her husband.

Dejected, Johnny would create an argument in order to engage his parents, which would end up in a fight. Underneath, his mother knew Johnny was feeling ignored so he'd spill over, but at the time she was too tired to make the choice to engage him in a meaningful way. Then one night she had an insight. She thought I may be too tired at night, but I can show Johnny more love in the morning.

The next morning, Johnny's mother appeared at the door of his bedroom with these words of wisdom. "Johnny, I owe you an apology. Each night you are so excited for me to watch you shoot hoops and I tell you the truth, your dad and I are tired. But I do want to watch and I do want to share in your joy. How about if we add "Morning Basketball" to our routine? We'll wake-up 15 minutes earlier until the end of the school year and shoot hoops together. I'll also make more of an effort to play games with you at night. I'll speak with your dad as well, we both want to be more present; it takes discipline and effort.

It can be difficult to cope with children who are over-the-top with emotional intensity. Our children can push our buttons, bringing up feelings of frustration, anger and helplessness. Our first step is to manage our own feelings, and even recognize our own part. Our children learn to manage their emotions by watching and listening to us. So the better we handle tough situations, with insight and problem-solving, the better our children will as well.

WHAT YOU CAN **SAY**

Your feelings matter to me, we can talk about how you feel.

Even though you are acting angry, I feel like you are sad and hurt. We can talk about that.

If our relationship were better, what would that look like to you?

What can we do together to be more peaceful?

Let's think about our energy level right now, are we needing to get some energy out?

When we bottle up our energy it can spill over, let's run in place and get some of that energy out.

Your anger is really BIG right now. What would help to shrink it down? Running? Jumping? Pushing against the walls?

You are angry. I can see how BIG your mad feelings are.

You're using BIG fighting words.

Would your mad feelings fill this room, our house, or blow the roof off?

Is your mad small, medium, large or SUPER-SIZED?

Are your mad feelings the size of a little puddle, a lake, a river, or an entire ocean?

If we name your feelings we can tame them.

In our family, it's okay to be mad, but it's not okay to be mean.

We can breathe in slowly for five seconds and out slowly for five seconds. This will calm us down.

Let's think of some ways you can say you're mad. What words do you think might work for you?

Perhaps it's time for some meditation music, that can help us both calm down.

WHAT YOU CAN **THINK**

My child is telling me he cannot handle his emotions right now.

My job is to show my child a better way to deal with strong feelings.

It's my job to help my child replace his over-the-top expression with words and behaviors that will serve him better.

My child is looking to me for a good example of how to handle frustration, anger and disappointment.

I won't let my own anger get the best of me.

I can be angry and still stay calm.

I do not need to match my child's emotional intensity.

My response will determine the outcome of this.

I'm able to handle whatever behavior my child throws my way.

I'm the person in the bigger body, with the bigger brain. I can deal with this.

This situation only has as much power over me as I give it.

I am showing my child how to handle uncomfortable emotions.

Helping my child identify if he needs to let his energy out or calm it down is a skill that will last a lifetime.

Simply helping my child name his energy state will bring him the power of awareness.

This challenging moment won't last forever.

This is the opportunity for me to consider my child's needs first.

I'm in charge of my own reaction.

I'll practice identifying and taking responsibility for my own feelings so I don't take them out on my child.

WHAT YOU CAN **DO**

Look at your part in the explosions, what can you do differently?

Choose not to have an emotional reaction to your child's intensity.

Offer to do an activity with your child, even something brief like taking the dog for a walk outside can shift the brain into a place of peace.

Know that as you model staying calm while you talk with your intense child, it shows your child he can do the same.

Breathe through your own anger and keep the volume on your voice down.

Model a sense of calm. If you keep your cool, your child has a better chance of doing the same.

Use a calming skill such as music, exercise, meditation or yoga yourself.

Manage your own reaction to best help your child.

Have a list of "let our energy-out" and "calm our energy down" activities ready to put into action.

Own your own feelings of upset. Do not let your feelings take control of you.

GETTING ON THE SAME PAGE

It may be helpful to think of this kind of behavior as a signal that your child has reached critical mass and is unable to cope. Like a volcano that is spewing, once started, some kids find it difficult to stop. Becoming a detective and looking at what underlies the yelling, helps us get to the heart of the matter. Our children can push our buttons sometimes. We may personalize their emotional intensity, often responding in kind. It is imperative that we remind ourselves that our children's behavior is a source of communication.

Our children's emotional expressions are often about unmet needs. Our role is to help. When we personalize, we become stuck and are of little use to our children or ourselves. When family yelling is out of control, sometimes parents need to take the time to get on the same page. Breathe, use a few of our "what to think" strategies and calm your own limbic system. This will help you keep in the right frame of mind to help your child.

> Don't personalize your child's behavior. He is not "doing something" to you; he is communicating with you. What does he most need from you when he's struggling with his feelings?

I PARENT SO DIFFERENTLY FROM MY SIGNIFICANT OTHER. NOW WHAT?

We have found that while parents often want the same things for their children (happiness, success, and a good moral compass) they may have different ideas of how this should be accomplished. This is akin to being in the same book, but on a different page. A clear example of this would be when one parent believes that consequences and punishment are the best way to raise decent human beings, while the other parent believes that listening, compassion and guidance will more quickly accomplish this goal. Clearly, there is a disconnect between the parents. The children in the family will sense this, which only adds to the confusion about "how" to "do the right thing."

This can be very challenging for families. It might help to know this is not an uncommon problem. This is especially true because most of us were raised in a society that values compliance at any cost and has a long-standing belief that consequences and punishment are the holy grail of behavior change. When we know better, we can do better. Neuroscientific research has shown us how antiquated and misguided a punitive model of childrearing is. We can now inform parenting and teaching practices by this relatively new knowledge. We know that lasting change is based upon the ideas we share in Bloom.

SHOULD WE KEEP PLAYING GOOD COP/BAD COP?

In some families, one parent may play the disciplinarian, while the other parent falls into the role of being the "easy" one. With Bloom, both parents get to be the "good guy". This is so because both parents are able to provide loving guidance, fairness, and can teach new skills. Kids flourish when they know that either parent can provide them with the "know how" to handle the tough stuff in life. When parents cannot agree, kids can sense this. Their subconscious mind believes, "You guys don't even know what to do about my behavior. How can I possibly behave if the two most important people in my life can't help me?" With Bloom, you have the know-how to help in meaningful ways.

IS GETTING ON THE SAME PAGE POSSIBLE WHEN WE CAN'T AGREE ON A PARENTING STYLE?

Get some clarity about what is most important to you as parents. This is true for parents who are still together, as well as for those who have chosen to part ways. If necessary, seek mediation or counseling to help you get on the same page. It will pay off a thousand times over. Get crystal clear about what you want for your child and then find common ground for how you will help your child grow in that direction. This is absolutely possible to attain. When your child knows the two of you are aligned in how to grow great children, they will BLOSSOM! We've seen it happen again and again.

UP TO CODE?

If you and your partner need extra help from each other to stay the course, develop a secret code to use that acts as a signal, "Hey, you take over here, I'm about to lose it!" This can go a long way towards success!

Some families accomplish this by using a scale. Jennifer and Jason rate issues and interactions on a scale from 1-5 with 1 meaning "get up off the couch and intervene now" and 5 meaning "it's all good no intervention needed." So when their kids break a rule they are able to communicate quickly using their "secret signal."

As an example, a recent sibling conflict was a "3" (let's let them work it out), while a text that read "Mom, I'll be home late," was a "I" because their teenaged son knew to be home by curfew and was pushing the limits.

Using a communication strategy that is quick and efficient such as a secret signal or a rating scale helps both parents get on the same page without a flurry of words that can often lead to miscommunication or even more anger.

ANGER MANAGEMENT STRATEGIES

One strategy we've found to be successful is called Anger Mountain. Anger Mountain is another way to explore what makes a child blow-up or melt-down. You can help your child explore what "What happened before the melt-down." "What did you see, hear or do that made you start to get angry?" "What did other people do that made you so frustrated, angry or sad?" In each colored box you can write what was going on that caused the escalation. Then on the right hand-side write ways the child could cope in the future to calm down. Writing or drawing how the outcome could have "looked differently" had the child used calming skills, helps your child plan future calming strategies.

Anger Mountain is flexible and can be adapted for your specific needs.

HOW IT WORKS

Imagine that a child climbs Anger Mountain (or it can also be Energy Mountain or Anxiety Mountain) when things do not go their way. Some children escalate very quickly. Other children can self-regulate and walk down the mountain without letting their anger become uncontrolled. Some children hang out near the top of Anger Mountain, feeling agitated, frustrated, anxious and annoyed. In fact, we have known children who climb up Anger Mountain, scream and yell and just simply fall apart and then are calm for days afterward (it's like a neurobiological reset flooding the body with endorphins).

Managing one's intense feelings is learned. Separating out what causes one to escalate (the event) and what they think or feel about the event (it's what we think and feel that makes us climb) is useful throughout a lifetime.

Anger Mountain

What made me feel this way

How I calmed down

On the Anger Mountain printable, we have three columns. On the left we have triggers that make us escalate, that includes what your child was thinking or feeling. In the middle we have colored boxes where the child can write key words describing what was happening as he escalated. On the right we have the activities or actions we can do to experience calm *(breathe, do yoga, walk backwards, ask for help)*. So literally, we are writing what made us climb Anger Mountain on the left side and what helped us calm down on the right.

On the left side of the mountain we write down thoughts and feelings that make us go from a sense of calm (blue) to agitated, annoyed, or frustrated (orange or red). Labeling different feelings and experiences as colors helps kids understand and communicate how they feel. "I feel happy and live in blue when I am playing with my friends or reading with Dad." "I feel bugged and green when Mom says stop what you are doing and come eat dinner." "I feel pink or a bit red when I get a sandwich I hate for lunch," and so on.

On the right side of the mountain we write down calming "skills" that could help us climb back down Anger Mountain before we explode. *"When I feel orange because my Mom told me I cannot go outside, I can play with my trains or go ride my bike."* The middle colored area is where we put key words like *"Don't take it personally." "Let my mind be flexible." "Choose another activity." "How I feel is my choice."* These are like little rescue sentences for the child's brain to hold on to instead of escalating.

With younger children, we tell them that their feelings are like a choo-choo train. Their train is happiest when it is "in the station." When their train is in the station, they feel calm, they enjoy playing, they have fun in family activities and they enjoy their friends. But, sometimes things happen that take our trains out of the station. A friend breaks our sand castle, or our mom says we have to put away our toys, or our sister calls our artwork "dumb." This makes our train rev up and zoom out of the station and up the mountain.

It doesn't have to about trains in a station… it could be flowers in the garden or fishies in the ocean. Any metaphor that suits your family will do. What you are doing for your child is giving them the thoughts, words and actions they can't find on their own.

Remember, Anger Mountain can be Anxiety Mountain, Frustration Mountain or even Depression Gulch. Change it to suit your family.

For a fresh approach at dealing with over-the-top emotions, check out the *"Anger Toolbox for Kids"* by Wendy Young. This anger management system for kids is unlike any other resource you've ever seen to help intense kids learn how to become successful in managing their feelings. Her website is *kidlutions.com*.

STORY-TELLING FOR MOOD MANAGEMENT

Now that you have been introspective, it's time to focus on teaching your child new skills. This is best done when your child is calm and receptive to learning new ideas. A critical aspect of learning how to manage one's emotions is understanding what leads up to the melt-down or explosion and how to get calm before you go over Anger Mountain and your volcano blows up. Using three-step stories with the beginning, middle and end of an experience is a helpful tool.

We already discussed the "Draw It Out" method of story telling. Now, we would like to introduce you to Polyspot Stories. In the case of feelings management, it is helpful for the child to break the story down and see what thoughts and feelings lead to overwhelm or exploding. With Polyspot Stories we move one step beyond describing the parts of the story to describing how you could re-write the story so that it has a happier ending next time.

Using the Polyspot Story Telling Method you and the child draw or write out:

» It all started when…

» Then you describe who said and or did what.

» Then you describe how the incident ended.

» Next you write or draw out what could be done differently next time.

» You preview and comment on what will happen next, when the new words, thoughts or actions are implemented.

» The story now has a happier ending, which you describe so that the child can imagine and explore how things can be better.

Polyspot Stories

It all started when   He did this, she did this....   How the story ended
                       I said this... I did this...

Polyspot Stories

Next time, I could do this   Then this will happen....   What a happier ending will look like

To make this come alive for your child, you can create the polyspots out of large circles of construction paper and lay them on the floor. Laminate or cover the polyspots in contact paper for durability. You can invite your child to literally jump from circle to circle, as they answer the questions that go with each polyspot. This provides an active way to think things through. When you engage your child's body and mind, your child has a complete experience with this activity and will tend to remember the concepts when he needs them most. Most of all, have fun with these creative interventions. If they don't go over well the first time, do not abandon them. Keep trying! You can even model how it works for your child.

THE FAMILY TANTRUM
OUR WHOLE FAMILY SEEMS OUT OF CONTROL. HOW DO WE GET IT BACK?

Even when we as parents perceive that our child escalated without warning, we have the power to impact the situation with our own responses. Our children do not "cause" us to join the tantrum or lose control. We do that because we feel overwhelmed, helpless or worn-out. Children can feel frightened when their parents seem out of control (emotionally or physically). The defensive brain takes over when a person feels attacked or afraid. Yelling quickly touches off the 'fight or flight' mechanism resulting in a "family tantrum." Keeping an eye on your own reactions truly helps.

What can you do in the moment?

1. Think before you move or speak.

2. Monitor your non-verbal communication. Consider what your face and posture say to your child.

3. Monitor your verbal tone. You may not mean to sound sarcastic, angry or contemptuous, but some of us do when our buttons are pushed.

4. Focus on breathing and calming down.

5. Regulate your own emotions, without taking them out on your children.

6. Ask for help. Sometimes emotion management means looking into the past to manage feelings better in the future.

7. If you tell your child you need space and time to get calm yourself, model doing it in a calm, mature manner. Sometimes parents say, "See how upset I am? I need my own time to calm down now," as though it's the child's fault. Managing our own emotions is our work, it is for us to do without blaming others for how we feel.

IN A NUTSHELL: WHAT MAKE US SPILL-OVER?

» A child may be bombarded and overwhelmed by the family's yelling or intense reactions.

» A child may have an intense temperament, which makes him have over-the-top responses. This child needs more help from his parents to modulate his emotions.

» One (or both) of the parents may have an intense temperament, which may set the emotional tone for the family.

» A child may get most of his attention with negative behavior.

» Kids have a way of commanding undivided attention when parents are emotionally unavailable.

» The stress level in the family may be high and this child simply acts as a barometer for that stress.

» Parents don't know how to help themselves, which makes it difficult for them to teach their children a better way.

» Responding in an intense manner may be a habit for the whole family.

» Loud yelling and even swearing may be the best way the child knows to get immediate attention.

» Learning new skills is something entire families can do. It's not always just our kids who need changing. We have to be courageous enough to look at ourselves in the mirror, so we can better help our children.

MORE RESOURCES

» *Cool Down and Work Through Anger* by Cheri J. Meiners M.Ed.

» *The Big Book of Parenting Solutions* by Michele Borba, EdD

» *The Explosive Child* by Ross Greene, PhD

» *No Bad Kids: Toddler Discipline Without Shame* by Janet Lansbury

» For more ideas, find the Anger Toolbox and Ice-Cream Cones and Frozen Pops at *kidlutions.com*

More tips from Wendy: Four Surprising Ways to Calm Down So Your Kids Can, Too

Your feelings matter to me, we can talk about how you feel.

BLOOM 50 Things To Say, Think, And Do With Anxious, Angry, and Over-the-Top Kids

Even though you are acting angry, I feel like you are sad and hurt. We can talk about that.

BLOOM 50 Things To Say, Think, And Do With Anxious, Angry, and Over-the-Top Kids

If our relationship were better, what would that look like to you?

BLOOM 50 Things To Say, Think, And Do With Anxious, Angry, and Over-the-Top Kids

What can we do together to be more peaceful?

BLOOM 50 Things To Say, Think, And Do With Anxious, Angry, and Over-the-Top Kids

Let's think about our energy level right now, are we needing to get some energy out?

BLOOM 50 Things To Say, Think, And Do With Anxious, Angry, and Over-the-Top Kids

When we bottle up our energy it can spill over, let's run in place and get some of that energy out.

BLOOM 50 Things To Say, Think, And Do With Anxious, Angry, and Over-the-Top Kids

SAY

Your anger is really BIG right now. What would help to shrink it down? Running? Jumping? Pushing against the walls?

SAY

You are angry. I can see how BIG your mad feelings are.

SAY

You're using BIG fighting words.

SAY

Would your mad feelings fill this room, our house, or blow the roof off?

SAY

Is your mad small, medium, large or SUPER-SIZED?

SAY

Are your mad feelings the size of a little puddle, a lake, a river, or an entire ocean?

SAY

If we name your feelings we can tame them.

BLOOM 50 Things To Say, Think, And Do With Anxious, Angry, and Over-the-Top Kids

SAY

In our family, it's okay to be mad, but it's not okay to be mean.

BLOOM 50 Things To Say, Think, And Do With Anxious, Angry, and Over-the-Top Kids

SAY

We can breathe in slowly for five seconds and out slowly for five seconds. This will calm us down.

BLOOM 50 Things To Say, Think, And Do With Anxious, Angry, and Over-the-Top Kids

SAY

Let's think of some ways you can say you're mad. What words do you think might work for you?

BLOOM 50 Things To Say, Think, And Do With Anxious, Angry, and Over-the-Top Kids

SAY

Perhaps it's time for some meditation music, that can help us both calm down.

BLOOM 50 Things To Say, Think, And Do With Anxious, Angry, and Over-the-Top Kids

SAY

BLOOM 50 Things To Say, Think, And Do With Anxious, Angry, and Over-the-Top Kids

THINK

My child is telling me he cannot handle his emotions right now.

BLOOM 50 Things To Say, Think, And Do With Anxious, Angry, and Over-the-Top Kids

THINK

My job is to show my child a better way to deal with strong feelings.

BLOOM 50 Things To Say, Think, And Do With Anxious, Angry, and Over-the-Top Kids

THINK

It's my job to help my child replace his over-the-top expression with words and behaviors that will serve him better.

BLOOM 50 Things To Say, Think, And Do With Anxious, Angry, and Over-the-Top Kids

THINK

My child is looking to me for a good example of how to handle frustration, anger and disappointment.

BLOOM 50 Things To Say, Think, And Do With Anxious, Angry, and Over-the-Top Kids

THINK

I won't let my own anger get the best of me.

BLOOM 50 Things To Say, Think, And Do With Anxious, Angry, and Over-the-Top Kids

THINK

I can be angry and still stay calm.

BLOOM 50 Things To Say, Think, And Do With Anxious, Angry, and Over-the-Top Kids

THINK

I do not need to match my child's emotional intensity.

BLOOM 50 Things To Say, Think, And Do With Anxious, Angry, and Over-the-Top Kids

THINK

My response will determine the outcome of this.

BLOOM 50 Things To Say, Think, And Do With Anxious, Angry, and Over-the-Top Kids

THINK

I'm able to handle whatever behavior my child throws my way.

BLOOM 50 Things To Say, Think, And Do With Anxious, Angry, and Over-the-Top Kids

THINK

I'm the person in the bigger body, with the bigger brain. I can deal with this.

BLOOM 50 Things To Say, Think, And Do With Anxious, Angry, and Over-the-Top Kids

THINK

This situation only has as much power over me as I give it.

BLOOM 50 Things To Say, Think, And Do With Anxious, Angry, and Over-the-Top Kids

THINK

I am showing my child how to handle uncomfortable emotions.

BLOOM 50 Things To Say, Think, And Do With Anxious, Angry, and Over-the-Top Kids

THINK

Helping my child identify if he needs to let his energy out or calm it down is a skill that will last a lifetime.

BLOOM 50 Things To Say, Think, And Do With Anxious, Angry, and Over-the-Top Kids

THINK

Simply helping my child name his energy state will bring him the power of awareness.

BLOOM 50 Things To Say, Think, And Do With Anxious, Angry, and Over-the-Top Kids

THINK

This challenging moment won't last forever.

BLOOM 50 Things To Say, Think, And Do With Anxious, Angry, and Over-the-Top Kids

THINK

This is the opportunity for me to consider my child's needs first.

BLOOM 50 Things To Say, Think, And Do With Anxious, Angry, and Over-the-Top Kids

THINK

I'm in charge of my own reaction.

BLOOM 50 Things To Say, Think, And Do With Anxious, Angry, and Over-the-Top Kids

THINK

I'll practice identifying and taking responsibility for my own feelings so I don't take them out on my child.

BLOOM 50 Things To Say, Think, And Do With Anxious, Angry, and Over-the-Top Kids

DO

Look at your part in the explosions, what can you do differently?

DO

Choose not to have an emotional reaction to your child's intensity.

DO

Offer to do an activity with your child, even something brief like taking the dog for a walk outside can shift the brain into a place of peace.

DO

Know that as you model staying calm while you talk with your intense child, it shows your child he can do the same.

DO

Breathe through your own anger and keep the volume on your voice down.

DO

Model a sense of calm. If you keep your cool, your child has a better chance of doing the same.

DO

Use a calming skill such as music, exercise, meditation or yoga yourself.

BLOOM 50 Things To Say, Think, And Do With Anxious, Angry, and Over-the-Top Kids

DO

Manage your own reaction to best help your child.

BLOOM 50 Things To Say, Think, And Do With Anxious, Angry, and Over-the-Top Kids

DO

Have a list of "let our energy-out" and "calm our energy down" activities ready to put into action.

BLOOM 50 Things To Say, Think, And Do With Anxious, Angry, and Over-the-Top Kids

DO

Own your own feelings of upset. Do not let your feelings take control of you.

BLOOM 50 Things To Say, Think, And Do With Anxious, Angry, and Over-the-Top Kids

DO

BLOOM 50 Things To Say, Think, And Do With Anxious, Angry, and Over-the-Top Kids

DO

BLOOM 50 Things To Say, Think, And Do With Anxious, Angry, and Over-the-Top Kids

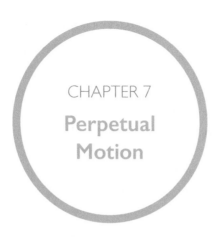

CHAPTER 7

Perpetual Motion

BUSY BODIES NEED TO MOVE

"My daughter faces potentially losing her spot in preschool because she cannot sit still. The teacher tells me she is constantly moving, which is a distraction to the rest of the class."

Frequently, children get into trouble at home and in school because they move too much. They fidget, fall off chairs, leave their seats, or are generally disruptive to the class. In this example we explore why kids move and what to do about it.

WHAT MAKES KIDS MOVE SO MUCH?

Children move at home and in the classroom for a variety of reasons. In our work, we have seen children move too much due to sensory overstimulation, hearing issues, vision problems and a variety of related concerns.

Neurobiological issues such as ADHD, learning differences, developmental lags, and delays in social-emotional development may also be factors. As we know from research, younger children in a classroom are diagnosed more with ADHD than their older peers.

We need to consider whether this is a developmental or biological issue. It might even be time to see your pediatrician, a developmental pediatrician or psychologist. Brain development happens over time and as the brain matures, children often gain better control of their attention, motor inhibition, and their emotional responses to social situations. In the meantime, some skillful intervention, better nutrition, and new strategies may be helpful.

SOME BEAUTIFUL CHILDREN SIMPLY NEED MOVEMENT TO THINK

Standing up, walking around, tapping one's pencil, and chewing on erasers are all ways that some children engage their brains. Movement engages the vestibular system in the body which helps maintain alertness and arousal through interaction with the reticular activating system (RAS). We know – big words – we think so too. But pretty darn cool, that movement can help us all focus. Ready for this? Your child's little movements actually release neurotransmitters such as dopamine that help the brain stay on-line. Pretty amazing, eh? In popular psychology, dopamine is often touted as the "feel good" neurotransmitter but it's better thought of as the "let's be alert to learn" neurotransmitter. There are over 100 neurotransmitters or "chemical messengers" identified. They are usually divided into inhibitory and or excitatory neurotransmitters such as serotonin, GABA, dopamine, noradrenaline and more. These neurotransmitters can have either an energizing or calming effect on the child. Many neurotransmitters are made from the food that you eat, Therefore, we will talk about eating good quality whole foods in just a bit.

Can you picture little ones who hang their tongues out while they write or move one arm too much as they run? This is a sign of a growing brain. When children do a novel task that is complex, they may recruit motor neurons. Doing so increases motor movement because they are expending a lot of energy thinking or executing the task. As the brain matures, some of these movements disappear. Other times however, the child's brain needs a little help. That is when we consider behavioral, learning, nutritional or medication interventions.

IN A NUTSHELL: WHAT MAKES KIDS MOVE?

The brain develops its movement centers before its thinking centers. In many ways, we move to think. Children also move to learn. For some children, movement stimulates the thinking centers of the brain. Amazing how biology knows what a child needs to think better.

REASONS KIDS NEED TO MOVE

The brain wants to fidget, doodle, and even dawdle, to stimulate the intelligence and creativity centers of the brain.

Lights, sounds, outside noises, smells, and over-crowded conditions can cause the child's sensory system to feel over-stimulated.

Classroom work can be at or below the child's cognitive level, causing them to move around seeking brain stimulation.

Classroom environments and teaching methods vary. Reflect on the emotional tone in the room, the physical environment, the attitude of the teacher and their specific methods of teaching (instruction, demonstration, activity). Do they match the learning style of your child?

Some children need to test the boundaries and limits in a classroom in order to familiarize themselves with classroom expectations. While many children listen to the limits and respond well, other children need to experience limits in order to respond to them. They are testing the boundaries and learning the expectations every time they change classrooms or teachers.

For some children, movement is an expression of their internal feelings. When worried, nervous, frustrated, angry or hurt, children move to express themselves.

For some children, moving is a sign of neurotransmitter imbalances that can be addressed by your physician or health care provider.

Bigger kids are expected to act older. Consider the individual characteristics of your child when compared with her classmates. Consider the age of your child with regard to the age of her peers. Is your child one of the younger classmates? Is your child tall for her age and therefore teachers expect more of her?

HOW CAN I HELP?

Be a detective. Consider how moving around is benefiting your child; Why does she need to move? We don't encourage you to force your child to stop fidgeting or moving because sometimes the brain requires movement to stay stimulated. In fact, we would love for you to consider whether your child may learn better while moving. We understand it can be frustrating for parents to have kids who cannot sit still and for teachers who have several squirmy movers in a classroom.

When it comes to fidgeting, it helps to be a detective, not a dictator. Talk with your child about her experience of fidgeting. Is your child aware she fidgets or moves a lot? Does your child feel she needs to fidget in order to get her energy out? Some kids will tell you their body feels almost prickly: Like they are popping with excitement. Is your child's need to fidget driven by sensations in her body? Does your child get up from circle time due to over or under stimulation? Maybe your child needs to be more involved in the classroom experience if being a passive listener is not yet part of her skill set.

We parents wish the best for our children. At times we feel embarrassed by their behavior. We perceive that others are telling us, "Make your child stop." Stopping the behavior is not our main goal. Transforming behavior with movement is our goal.

Here are some ideas on how to help your little mover slow down, calm down and be more successful at home and school.

WHAT YOU CAN **SAY**

I heard you had the 'wiggles' and were feeling fidgety today.

It can be hard for you to sit still in class.

Is it possible the other children are sitting too close to you? Do you need more space?

Do you notice that your body moves a lot?

Do you know when you are going to get out of your seat or does it just happen?

Do you feel that your body needs to wiggle, like you have a lot of energy?

Moving around feels better to you, doesn't it?

I know it can be hard to keep your body still when you're thinking so much. It means your brain is working.

Sometimes your body says, 'Get up,' and your teacher says, 'Sit down.'

You need to wait to get up when the teacher says it's time. Don't get up just because you want to.

There are times we need to sit still, shall we practice what that feels like?

Let's think about what your body needs to be able to sit still, when needed.

When it feels hard to sit still, tell your teacher you need help.

We can talk with your teacher about keeping your body busy so you can sit longer.

We can ask your teacher if you can keep fidget toys at your desk to help you stay alert.

Sometimes we move a lot to express our feelings.

Sometimes when we hold our feelings in, our bodies want to move.

"You must be proud of yourself for paying attention to the messages your body gives you."

"What do you feel inside when you move around a lot?"

"If your teacher asks you to stay still does that help you stay in your seat?"

"It's okay that you like to move, let's just choose the right time to get up and move around."

"Are there moments when you want to tap your pencil or draw on your paper to let your feelings come out?"

WHAT YOU CAN **THINK**

I need to understand the meaning of my child's behavior.

My child's behavior is goal-directed. What is she needing that she is not getting?

There is a reason my child needs to get up, walk around or move a lot.

How is moving around helping my child?

What might my child need that she cannot find when seated?

I wonder if other children in the class also need to get up more frequently.

Perhaps I can speak with the teacher about allowing my daughter to walk around a bit between centers or activities.

Might my child need to have more movement opportunities?

How can we add more movement into my child's day?

Is my child getting enough exercise?

Should we consider more trips to the park or playground outside of school?

How can I provide more stimulation to my child at her seat, so that her brain is engaged?

Might brain breaks like those provided by sparkpe.org help?

WHAT YOU CAN **DO**

Learn about mindfulness for children, being mindful of what their body feels like doing empowers a child to take positive action.

Mindfulness can be a big word for children. Simply put, mindfulness is awareness. Helping your child notice or observe their feelings, bodily sensations and thoughts *right now, in this very moment*, improves self-awareness leading to more active choices about behavior.

Write a list of things your child can do to release energy before, during and after school so that she can alternate being still and moving around.

Enlist the teacher's help. There are more times to move in classrooms than we often know. What your child may need are more scheduled movement breaks.

Talk to the school psychologist or occupational therapist at the school and use some sensory tools to help your child focus such as sitting discs, pillow chairs, resistive hand or foot bands, which provide your child proprioceptive feedback to help the brain stay online.

Ask the teacher, school psychologist, or occupational therapist if a ball chair might be helpful to your child. Sometimes using the core muscles of the body for balance decreases the need to get up and move around when it's not yet time to do so.

Help your child become her body's best teacher. When your body tells you it needs to move, you can listen and tell your body, we will get up and walk after the teacher is finished with the story.

Help your child recognize her energy states: When does she feel calm, when does her body have a lot of energy she needs to release?

Role play! Getting out of your seat looked like this, it could have looked like this (model alternate strategy), let's practice. Model the behavior of getting calm and staying calm for your child.

Get learning, thinking, planning and calming.

HERE ARE THREE BOOKS YOU MIGHT ENJOY.

Taking Charge of ADHD, Third Edition: The Complete, Authoritative Guide for Parents by Russell Barkley, PhD

Raising a Sensory Smart Child: The Definitive Handbook for Helping Your Child with Sensory Processing Issues by Lindsey Biel & Nancy Peske

A Moving Child is A Learning Child by Gill Connell and Cheryl McCarthy

HERE ARE A FEW WEBSITES THAT MIGHT HELP.

TherapyShoppe.com

funandfunction.com

additudemag.com

aota.org

We appreciate the calming music and stories from Lori Lite at *stressfreekids.com.*

For quality children's music to enhance learning and attachment check out *kiboomukidssongs.com*

PREVIEWING HELPS

In the most effective classrooms, teachers review the beginning, middle, and end of any upcoming action. It would look something like this:

"We are going to sit on the carpet and read, 'The Little Engine That Could.'" "When I raise my hands with our 'Let's move signal', we can then get up and walk to our centers."

"Now tell me class, let's say it out-loud, what are we going to do when we come to the carpet?"

Having the class repeat the steps reminds the brain "there is an order to this action and I need to follow it." Being ready to employ calming strategies like yoga, meditation, mindful breathing or soothing music may also be helpful. Other times, getting up and vigorously moving may be the answer. Both ends of the continuum can be helpful to think about. Keep in mind; it is normal for young children to move around a lot. The skill of learning to sit still comes with practice and maturity.

Actions like marching, walking, climbing, jumping, skipping and such are an integral part of brain development. Movement helps the two sides of the brain communicate and lay down connections. The more neural connections a child has, the better. All of this culminates in a brain that is best prepared to learn, think and grow. If you are looking for movement activities your child can do in the classroom *actionbasedlearning.com* and *sparkpe.org* are two helpful places to begin.

Kids feel the need to move for a reason. It is good for their bodies and their brains. We should all be in the business of trying to find ways to support movement to enhance learning.

GET YOUR "MOVE ON"

Fidgeting, moving and squirming is a personal experience. For some kids, we need to help them sit still to focus. Yet others need to move to focus, so it is important to look into strategies that suit each child as an individual. For many children, moving actually helps them think better. If this is the case, allow your child to draw, doodle or sit on a "Disc O Sit" designed to give the body sensory input while seated. Also check to see if the child's seat is ergonomic or capable of movement. For occupational therapy-style products visit abilitations.com or therapyshoppe.com. For play therapy toys visit playtherapysupply.com. Research them and see what suits your child.

Providing a specific focus for the extra energy can help. For example, providing a portable patch of fabric the child can put in a pocket and rub to calm themselves can be very helpful. In your new role as a detective, ask if she would prefer her "touch pad" to be smooth, like silk, or scratchy like Velcro. You could even propose different focal points for her energy on different days, to keep her brain interested. Kid Companions also provides sensory pieces that are smooth and/ or bumpy for the child to discretely touch, while sitting in circle time or at a desk.

You may need to talk with the teacher and ask if your child can get up and walk to the back of the classroom and stand for a few minutes. Of course, it would be awesome if the teacher would let all the kids do a few yoga moves or stand to stretch in between academic activities. Classrooms where the children do not simply sit all day may be more suitable to your child. If more help is needed, consult an occupational therapist regarding classroom equipment.

As pediatric physical therapist, Shelley Mannell, tells us, sitting on an exercise ball, stool or even standing has been shown to help kids who are squirmy think better. Maybe the old-fashioned school chair or flat carpet square is not a good answer for your child.

Practice sitting still. Maybe your child isn't used to what it feels like not to move. Twice a day ask your child to sit still for 20 seconds, and then give a cheer to celebrate. Make it a game by asking them to play statue, freezing completely still. When the 20 seconds are up, have a special handshake or high-five! Now, let your child tell you when to freeze. Your child will learn from seeing you do it and they will enjoy feeling some mastery over the learning experience.

MUSIC AND RHYTHM FOR CALMING AND BRAIN DEVELOPMENT

It is said that music soothes the savage beast, but it might surprise you to also know that music can take the place of pharmaceuticals in some instances. A melody that is just as powerful as a pill? It's true, and research at Stanford has supported this notion. When kids have engines that are revved up, the right kind of music can get things back to a state of calm.

Music helps the mind calm down, focus better and become primed for learning. Alpha brainwaves inspired by music put us in a state of relaxed calm. This drug-free kind of intervention is completely accessible and reachable to all of our students in every school. Music really can be the best medicine!

For further reading on the use of musical rhythm to calm the mind, check out stronginstitute.com for starters. You can also search "binaural beats" online, for more insights. While more research is warranted in this area, the findings we currently have are promising. For more read, Healing at the Speed of Sound by Don Campbell & Alex Doman. Visit Advanced Brain Technologies for their new inTime program to learn about the role rhythm and timing play in brain development.

FOOD MATTERS

What you eat and what you feed your children really matters and may greatly impact movement that may be labeled "hyperactive". If your child is neuro-atypical or simply prone to excessive movement, inattention, over-the-top feelings, mood swings, anxiety, agitation, anger or sadness, shifting your nutrition habits away from processed food and toward whole food helps.

As parents, we are fortunate that there are many good resources to help us feed our families real nutrition. Here, we give you some tips and resources to begin getting your family back on track.

1. Eat dinner for breakfast. Having your children begin their day with quality protein, grains and healthy fats while limiting simple carbohydrates will fuel their bodies for hours. Instead of starting with pancakes and waffles, begin instead with turkey, meatballs, chicken, stir-fry or grass-fed beef lasagna. That's right, shoot for foods that provide 10 grams or more of protein per serving.

2. Sprinkle omega-3s throughout your day. A drizzle of olive oil, a handful of walnuts, a sprinkle of ground chia or flax seeds can fuel the body for work, school, and better thinking. Fish is also an excellent source of healthy fats. You can visit pathways4health.org for information on where to buy quality fish and grass-fed beef.

3. Go green. Be it in a salad, on a sandwich, or in a smoothie, eating handfuls of spinach, kale, arugula and colored vegetables helps the body fight stress. Think your child won't eat these things? Think again! If you need a little help with transitioning your kids to healthier foods, we highly recommend you pay a visit to Angelle Batten, M.Ed., at *angellebatten.com.* Your whole family will feel better for it!

4. Buy and eat foods that rot and sprout, "If it doesn't rot or sprout do without." *Clean Eating For Busy Families* by Michelle Dudash, R.D., *The Ultramind Solution* by Mark Hyman, MD and *The Eat Clean Diet* by Tosca Reno can help you get back to real food.

5. Hydrate ~ 1 oz. of clean water per pound of body weight per day.

6. Snack on fruits, vegetables, healthy fats and proteins throughout the day. Kids who have waffles for breakfast and crackers with juice for a snack are not eating brain food. Print out our healthy grocery list on the next page. Check out the *Harvard Food Pyramid.*

7. Eat a balanced diet. Nutrients come in many nature-made foods. Variety is good for your body.

Some children need to eat high quality fats and proteins every two-three hours to fuel their body. In this case, a few nuts or even an ounce of chicken or cheese is suitable.

REGISTERED DIETICIAN CHRISTY WILSON REMINDS US:

1. Shop in-season

2. Avoid the name brand stuff

3. Remember, fresh is always best

4. Only buy what you need for the week

5. Buy from your farmer's market

Here are some more sites we visit often.

happyfamilybrands.com

angrymoms.org

chefann.com

neurologicalhealth.org

littlejots.com

nourishinteractive.com

christywilsonnutrition.com

realmomnutrition.com

kidkritics.com

lawrencerosenmd.com

Here is Dr. Lynne's Whole Food Grocery List (It's just a start. Add what your kids love. Print it out, post it up and eat well.)

WHOLE FOODS GROCERY LIST

1.	Almond butter	36.	Kalamata olives	65.	Quinoa
2.	Almonds	37.	Kale	66.	Radishes
3.	Almond milk	38.	Kefir (great for	67.	Raisins
4.	Amaranth flakes		shakes)	68.	Raspberries
	(cereal)	39.	Laura's lean beef	69.	Rhubarb
5.	Apples		hamburger	70.	Rice crackers
6.	Avocados	40.	Lemon	71.	Rice noodles
7.	Bananas	41.	Lentils	72.	Romaine lettuce
8.	Black beans	42.	Limes	73.	Salmon
9.	Blueberries	43.	Low fat organic	74.	Salsa
10.	Broccoli		cottage cheese	75.	Seaweed
11.	Brown rice	44.	Low sodium soy	76.	Sesame Oil
12.	Buckwheat pancakes		sauce	77.	Sesame seeds
13.	Cabbage	45.	Mozzarella cheese	78.	Shallots
14.	Calcium fortified	46.	Mustard	79.	Sour cream
	orange juice	47.	Navy beans	80.	Sparkling water
15.	Cauliflower	48.	Okra	81.	Spelt bread
16.	Carrots	49.	Old fashioned	82.	Spinach
17.	Celery		oatmeal	83.	Sprouted wheat
18.	Corn tortillas	50.	Olive oil		bread
19.	Cranberries	51.	Olives	84.	Sprouts
20.	Cucumbers	52.	Onion	85.	Strawberries
21.	Eggplant	53.	Organic eggs (free	86.	Sweet potatoes
22.	Eggs		range)	87.	Tomato sauce
23.	Ezekiel bread	54.	Organic lean beef	88.	Tomatoes, diced,
24.	Fish		(free range)		organic
25.	Flax seeds	55.	Organic chicken	89.	Tomatoes, stewed,
26.	Garbanzo beans		(free range)		organic
27.	Garlic	56.	Organic milk	90.	Walnuts
28.	Ginger	57.	Organic turkey	91.	Water chestnuts
29.	Grapefruit juice	58.	Organic yogurt	92.	Wheat-berry bread
30.	Green beans	59.	Peas	93.	White beans
31.	Green tea	60.	Pears	94.	Whole fruit jams
32.	Guacamole	61.	Pecans	95.	Yams
33.	Honey	62.	Pinto beans	96.	Zucchini
34.	Hummus	63.	Plums		
35.	Jasmine rice	64.	Pumpkin		

ARE YOUR CHILD'S NEUROTRANSMITTERS ONLINE? NEUROWHAT?

It's important to know that our behavior can be a reflection of how our brains are functioning. Some children's neurotransmitters may be out-of-balance, contributing to over-the-top, anxious, angry, or depressed behavior. For some children, assessing their neurotransmitter function is a first step prior to a medication evaluation or implementing a behavior management plan.

Neurotransmitters are the brain chemicals that communicate information throughout our brain and body. They relay signals between nerve cells, called "neurons." Neurotransmitters can affect behavior, mood modulation, self-regulation, aggression, sleep, attention, weight and more. When neurotransmitter levels are depleted or imbalanced our brains and bodies do not function as well as we wish.

Genetics, diet, environmental factors, illnesses and hormones can all impact neurotransmitter function. Some physicians support neurotransmitter assessment, others do not. As with any test or treatment you may read the research and determine with the help of a medical professional what suits your child best. Here are a few resources, if you wish to learn more about neurotransmitter function, hormones, food, exercise and behavior:

Emily Roberts, LPC, MA is a valued resource at *neurogistics.com* as is clinical nutritionist Jan Katzen, who studies the biochemical bases of food and how nutrition impacts behavior. Laurie Dupar Senior Certified ADHD Coach and trained mental health nurse practitioner at *coachingforadhd.com* has an informative audio series on medication and ADHD, we find really helpful.

If your child has trouble getting going in the morning consider what your child might tell you…

Neurotransmitters are largely responsible for my behavior, attitude and energy. When I am slow to get going, distracted or resistant, it's often **NOT** simply a behavioral choice, it's biochemical.

EVEN MORE RESOURCES

True Food by Andrew Weil and Sam Fox

What Your Doctor May Not Tell You About Depression by Michael Schachter, M.D.

Gut and Psychology Syndrome: Natural Treatment for Autism, Dyspraxia, A.D.D., Dyslexia, A.D.H.D., Depression, Schizophrenia by Natasha Campbell-McBride

Spark: The Revolutionary New Science of Exercise and the Brain by John Ratey & Eric Hagerman

The 21 Day Belly Fix by Tasneem Bhatia, MD

A FEW FINAL THOUGHTS...

It is normal, natural and typical for young children to move a lot. After all, we move to grow our brains. Brain development is "bottom up" meaning that we connect our neurons by moving, doing and experiencing through movement. So if your child is a mover, consider her needs: What is she needing but not getting and how can you make her more aware of when she needs to move and when it's best to sit still? You may also consider the type of classroom your child is in. Some classrooms require sitting still all day long. For a child who is a mover, a developmental classroom or Montessori may be a better fit.

Adding several periods of movement to your child's day can help as well. A nice long walk before you head off to school, sports or yoga after school and plenty of movement after dinner can fuel your child's brain. It's really not about "stopping" it's about re-allocating your energy to times when it is appropriate to move.

MORE ON HOW TO ACTUALLY BE A BEHAVIORAL DETECTIVE

(Adapted from *The Family Coach Method*, St Lynn's Press, 2009)

Whenever a parent, teacher, care provider, or family member is seeking to solve a behavioral, developmental, social or learning issue, the best thing to do first is to take an inventory: Step back, watch, listen, observe and learn. Be calm, breathe through it, you'll see more clearly.

Before you intervene around a behavioral challenge or an issue at home or school, it's really important to step back, look at it objectively and understand the who, what, where, when, how, and why, of the specific behavior.

While many parents we meet come to talk about discipline, before we talk about behavioral interventions to increase collaboration, we discuss how to be a detective. Being a detective allows you to observe your parenting interactions a little differently. We learn to seek to understand before we intervene.

The problem with intervening too soon is that you might be implementing the mentality of "ready, fire, aim" instead of "ready, aim, fire."

Now of course, if you fire before you aim, chances are you're going to miss the mark and you're going to need to re-do the intervention. You may also have to undo your mistakes surrounding the original misfire. Worry not, for you can. But if you understand what you are doing and why, before you take action, you are more likely to hit the mark.

When you are a behavioral detective you are empowered to better understand the meaning of your child's behavior by considering the who, what, when, where and how of any specific behavior.

By being a detective you will learn to ask yourself:

Who was there?
What did I expect?
What did I get?
What did I understand?
What did I not understand?
What was my child trying to communicate to me?
What was going on in the environment?

What was happening?

What was my child doing?

What was I doing?

What were other people in the setting doing?

What time of day was it?

What happened before, during and after the specific behavior?

What was said?

What actions took place?

When did the behavior occur?

When did I respond? Did I wait too long? Could I have intervened to help sooner?

Where were we?

Where were the other family members?

Where were the other children in the classroom, playing field or setting?

How did I intervene?

How could I have said something differently?

How could I have done something differently?

HOW TO BE A BEHAVIORAL DETECTIVE IN 4 EASY STEPS

STEP 1: Reflect on the misbehavior in clear simple terms.

The ABCs of Being a Detective

In order to be a behavioral detective, take out a blank piece of paper and divide it into four columns. Observe, take notes and learn how to look at behavior from a new viewpoint.

In Column #1 describe the situation, behavior, experience or circumstance that posed a challenge for the child.

Some examples include:

» Mary would not do her homework
» Jennifer wouldn't eat what was served for dinner
» James couldn't sit still in school
» Rebecca wouldn't stay in her car seat
» Jamison kept picking on the same child in school

STEP 2: Note the situation that lead up to the misbehavior. Who was there, what was asked of the child, what was expected? What lead up to the behavior? What were the circumstances surrounding the experience?

Column #2 is labeled "A": What leads up to the behavior, what's going on at the time, who's present at the time, and what are the circumstances prior to the behavior. Notes in this column include:

- » Has the child eaten well?
- » Has the child slept well?
- » Does the child know the rules and expectations around the behavior?
- » Was the child prepared for the requested behavior or personal experience?
- » Did the child have a late-afternoon snack?
- » Was a parent impatient, thus contributing to the misbehavior?
- » Were there too many children in the classroom this morning, so that the class was loud or unruly?
- » Was the child woken up too early?
- » Was there an adult present to help the child with a skill deficit?
- » Did the child have the necessary skills to manage the experience?

STEP 3: Describe the actual behavior, duration and severity.

Column #3 is labeled "B": The actual behavior, its length, duration, severity.

In this column describe the specific behavior.

- » What happened?
- » What behavior was exhibited?
- » How long did it last?
- » How severe was the behavior?

STEP 4: Describe the outcome. What did you do, what did the child, tween or teen do? How did you intervene? How did the situation end?

Column #4 is labeled "C": How did the event end, what happened next, what were the consequences of the behavior, what did the child or other children around the child do, what were the interventions, how did each of those interventions work or not work. What was the resolution?

In this column describe who did what when and what were the resulting actions or consequences.

- » Who was there?
- » Who was involved?
- » What did each person say?
- » What did each person do?
- » What happened next?
- » Were consequences employed?
- » Was discipline used?
- » What form of discipline?
- » How was it administered?
- » By whom?
- » How did the child respond?
- » What seemed to work well?
- » What did not work well?
- » What improvements might be needed?

The next time your child misbehaves, become a behavioral detective. Sit back and observe. Take notes. Consider what you said and did. Consider what your child said and did. Consider what others said and did. Just being aware will likely alter your behavior as well as the behavior of your child.

You'll be amazed by what you learn. Just looking, listening and learning changes behavior, watch. When you understand the who, what, when, where and how of your child's behavior you can make more informed choices regarding how to intervene.

More tips from Lynne: Three Secrets Teachers
Need to Know About Kids Who Move Too Much

SAY

I heard you had the 'wiggles' and were feeling fidgety today.

SAY

It can be hard for you to sit still in class.

SAY

Is it possible the other children are sitting too close to you? Do you need more space?

SAY

Do you notice that your body moves a lot?

SAY

Do you know when you are going to get out of your seat or does it just happen?

SAY

Do you feel that your body needs to wiggle, like you have a lot of energy?

SAY

Moving around feels better to you, doesn't it?

BLOOM 50 Things To Say, Think, And Do With Anxious, Angry, and Over-the-Top Kids

SAY

I know it can be hard to keep your body still when you're thinking so much. It means your brain is working.

BLOOM 50 Things To Say, Think, And Do With Anxious, Angry, and Over-the-Top Kids

SAY

Sometimes your body says, 'Get up,' and your teacher says, 'Sit down.'

BLOOM 50 Things To Say, Think, And Do With Anxious, Angry, and Over-the-Top Kids

SAY

You need to wait to get up when the teacher says it's time. Don't get up just because you want to.

BLOOM 50 Things To Say, Think, And Do With Anxious, Angry, and Over-the-Top Kids

SAY

There are times we need to sit still, shall we practice what that feels like?

BLOOM 50 Things To Say, Think, And Do With Anxious, Angry, and Over-the-Top Kids

SAY

Let's think about what your body needs to be able to sit still, when needed.

BLOOM 50 Things To Say, Think, And Do With Anxious, Angry, and Over-the-Top Kids

SAY

When it feels hard to sit still, tell your teacher you need help.

BLOOM 50 Things To Say, Think, And Do With Anxious, Angry, and Over-the-Top Kids

SAY

We can talk with your teacher about keeping your body busy so you can sit longer.

BLOOM 50 Things To Say, Think, And Do With Anxious, Angry, and Over-the-Top Kids

SAY

We can ask your teacher if you can keep fidget toys at your desk to help you stay alert.

BLOOM 50 Things To Say, Think, And Do With Anxious, Angry, and Over-the-Top Kids

SAY

Sometimes we move a lot to express our feelings.

BLOOM 50 Things To Say, Think, And Do With Anxious, Angry, and Over-the-Top Kids

SAY

Sometimes when we hold our feelings in, our bodies want to move.

BLOOM 50 Things To Say, Think, And Do With Anxious, Angry, and Over-the-Top Kids

SAY

You must be proud of yourself for paying attention to the messages your body gives you.

BLOOM 50 Things To Say, Think, And Do With Anxious, Angry, and Over-the-Top Kids

What do you feel inside when you move around a lot?

BLOOM 50 Things To Say, Think, And Do With Anxious, Angry, and Over-the-Top Kids

If your teacher asks you to stay still does that help you stay in your seat?

BLOOM 50 Things To Say, Think, And Do With Anxious, Angry, and Over-the-Top Kids

It's okay that you like to move, let's just choose the right time to get up and move around.

BLOOM 50 Things To Say, Think, And Do With Anxious, Angry, and Over-the-Top Kids

Are there moments when you want to tap your pencil or draw on your paper to let your feelings come out?

BLOOM 50 Things To Say, Think, And Do With Anxious, Angry, and Over-the-Top Kids

BLOOM 50 Things To Say, Think, And Do With Anxious, Angry, and Over-the-Top Kids

BLOOM 50 Things To Say, Think, And Do With Anxious, Angry, and Over-the-Top Kids

THINK

I need to understand the meaning of my child's behavior.

BLOOM 50 Things To Say, Think, And Do With Anxious, Angry, and Over-the-Top Kids

THINK

My child's behavior is goal-directed. What is she needing that she is not getting?

BLOOM 50 Things To Say, Think, And Do With Anxious, Angry, and Over-the-Top Kids

THINK

There is a reason my child needs to get up, walk around or move a lot.

BLOOM 50 Things To Say, Think, And Do With Anxious, Angry, and Over-the-Top Kids

THINK

How is moving around helping my child?

BLOOM 50 Things To Say, Think, And Do With Anxious, Angry, and Over-the-Top Kids

THINK

What might my child need that she cannot find when seated?

BLOOM 50 Things To Say, Think, And Do With Anxious, Angry, and Over-the-Top Kids

THINK

I wonder if other children in the class also need to get up more frequently.

BLOOM 50 Things To Say, Think, And Do With Anxious, Angry, and Over-the-Top Kids

THINK

Perhaps I can speak with the teacher about allowing my daughter to walk around a bit between centers or activities.

BLOOM 50 Things To Say, Think, And Do With Anxious, Angry, and Over-the-Top Kids

THINK

Might my child need to have more movement opportunities?

BLOOM 50 Things To Say, Think, And Do With Anxious, Angry, and Over-the-Top Kids

THINK

How can we add more movement into my child's day?

BLOOM 50 Things To Say, Think, And Do With Anxious, Angry, and Over-the-Top Kids

THINK

Is my child getting enough exercise?

BLOOM 50 Things To Say, Think, And Do With Anxious, Angry, and Over-the-Top Kids

THINK

Should we consider more trips to the park or playground outside of school?

BLOOM 50 Things To Say, Think, And Do With Anxious, Angry, and Over-the-Top Kids

THINK

How can I provide more stimulation to my child at her seat, so that her brain is engaged? Might brain breaks like those provided by sparkpe.org help?

BLOOM 50 Things To Say, Think, And Do With Anxious, Angry, and Over-the-Top Kids

DO

Learn about mindfulness for children, being mindful of what their body feels like doing empowers a child to take positive action.

DO

Helping your child notice or observe their feelings, bodily sensations and thoughts *right now, in this very moment,* improves self-awareness leading to more active choices about behavior.

DO

Write a list of things your child can do to release energy before, during and after school so that she can alternate being still and moving around.

DO

Enlist the teacher's help. There are more times to move in classrooms than we often know. What your child may need are more scheduled movement breaks.

DO

Talk to the school psychologist or occupational therapist at the school and use some sensory tools to help your child focus.

DO

Ask the teacher, school psychologist, or occupational therapist if a ball chair might be helpful to your child.

DO

Help your child become her body's "best teacher."

BLOOM 50 Things To Say, Think, And Do With Anxious, Angry, and Over-the-Top Kids

DO

"When your body tells you it needs to move, you can listen and tell your body, "we will get up and walk after the teacher is finished with the story."

BLOOM 50 Things To Say, Think, And Do With Anxious, Angry, and Over-the-Top Kids

DO

Help your child recognize her energy states: When does she feel calm, when does her body have a lot of energy she needs to release?

BLOOM 50 Things To Say, Think, And Do With Anxious, Angry, and Over-the-Top Kids

DO

Role play! "Getting out of your seat looked like this, it could have looked like this (model alternate strategy), let's practice."

BLOOM 50 Things To Say, Think, And Do With Anxious, Angry, and Over-the-Top Kids

DO

Model the behavior of getting calm and staying calm for your child.

BLOOM 50 Things To Say, Think, And Do With Anxious, Angry, and Over-the-Top Kids

DO

BLOOM 50 Things To Say, Think, And Do With Anxious, Angry, and Over-the-Top Kids

CHAPTER 8

Schoolhouse Blues

BETTER BEHAVIOR BLUEPRINT

"It has become really stressful when my phone rings, because it is usually my seven-year-old's teacher. He is having such a hard time behaving in school. He gets up from his desk, bothers other children and can be bossy toward his teacher. We have had school meetings. Once, I even took him to therapy but now I need more help."

WHY DON'T KIDS JUST BEHAVE AT SCHOOL?

Many issues may underlie complicated behavior in school. It could be difficulty with executive function, social skills, academic skills, interpersonal skills, body management skills, teacher-child fit, developmental level, or something else. Young children are just learning how to manage difficult feelings and situations. They may lack an appropriate way to express what they need. They communicate their feelings of upset with misguided behavior. This is a clue that your child needs more help. Remember, punishment will do nothing to assist them in making a better choice next time. They will still be at a loss about how to handle difficult feelings and situations unless you show them a better way.

WE TEACH RESPECT AND KINDNESS AT HOME. WHY CAN'T MY CHILD DISPLAY THESE BEHAVIORS AT SCHOOL?

Young children may display undesirable behaviors because they cannot convey in words their academic, interpersonal or sensory experiences. They may feel over-stimulated or overwhelmed in the classroom environment. Sometimes these behaviors come out as transgressions against peers. In other instances, children may be generally disruptive to the classroom because they have attention, concentration or impulsivity issues. All behaviors tell us what words cannot, or do not.

WHAT CAN PARENTS AND TEACHERS DO ABOUT THIS?

One of the most important things parents and teachers can do is recognize challenging behaviors as a skill-deficit. Generally, this includes difficulties with self-regulation, thinking and impulse control. Skill-deficits may lead to feelings of confusion, overwhelm or inadequacy. These feelings interfere with the child's every day functioning. Lacking better alternatives, children downshift into their emotional brain. Their behavior is signaling, "I need help! Please give me the thoughts, words and behaviors to succeed at school." There is hope! Self-regulation is a skill that can be taught. The future is bright! Your patience and calm guidance will help your child modulate their feelings sooner rather than later.

WHAT IS MISBEHAVIOR A SIGN OF?

One of the most critical things to bear in mind is that misbehavior in a child is not indicative of a "bad kid". It may simply be a sign that the child does not have the skills to meet the task demands in the classroom, on the playground, or at home. We need to ask why.

Does your child have difficulty with any of the following: Paying attention, monitoring their time, making appropriate choices, being still, reading social cues, understanding spoken language, reading, writing or inhibiting their impulses? The list goes on. As a parent (teacher), you need to uncover specifically what your child is having difficulty doing.

As a society, we tend to treat the misbehavior rather than the underlying skill deficit. This is a disservice to everyone involved. In addition to using Bloom, it can be wise to seek a comprehensive evaluation by a qualified specialist.

WHO CAN WE SEE?

Developmental Pediatrician
Functional/Integrative Medicine Physician
Family Physician
Occupational Therapist

Pediatrician

School Psychologist

Child Neuropsychologist

Pediatric Physical Therapist

Audiologist

Speech/language Therapist

Psychologist

Counselor

Therapist

Teacher

Social Worker

Nutritionist

HOW CAN THEY HELP?

When you first notice that your child has difficulty with development, language, academics, social skills or behavior, it's difficult to know where to begin. You can choose to start with an evaluation by your pediatrician or family physician in order to identify the "domain of referral." Your physician will then refer you to the proper specialist.

If the child has a developmental issue, a psychologist or early interventionist can help. If the issue is communication, language skills, or social skills, a speech therapist may be best. If the issue appears to be attention, distractibility or impulsivity a child neuropsychologist, psychologist or developmental pediatrician is a helpful start. In the domain of academics, a school psychologist or child neuropsychologist can assess for cognitive skill deficits or learning disabilities and recommend the appropriate intervention.

WHAT IS AN INTERVENTION?

An intervention is a treatment such as varying kinds of therapy: Speech-language therapy, occupational therapy, play therapy, cognitive-behavior therapy and others are designed to increase skill sets for optimal functioning.

Beginning the intervention process with a data-based evaluation helps you match the child's challenges with the best intervention.

Imagine this: You notice your child is having behavioral difficulty in school, so you call a trusted friend and ask for a referral. Your friend's child saw a play therapist they adored so she gives you the number. You call, do twelve sessions of play therapy and it improves things. Your child appears more optimistic and happier. But you still wonder, "What is underneath my child's misbehavior?" "Why are they having such a hard time behaving in school?" This is exactly why we begin with quality assessment before we choose an intervention when possible. "What was effective for your friend's child may not be exactly what is most effective for yours."

In our practices, we have referred children with behavior difficulty for brief neuropsychological testing only to learn that the child was gifted, had dyslexia, or had a pragmatic language deficit. A child like this may benefit from psychotherapy, but they may also need another level of intervention. **When we know more we can do better.**

While we prefer data-based interventions that begin with quality assessment, testing can be expensive. Asking for data relevant to your child by providing your school, neuropsychologist, psychologist or developmental pediatrician with well-thought-out referral questions can save time and money.

Not every child needs a complete neuropsychology test battery or psycho-educational evaluation in order to provide data relevant to intervention or treatment planning. If you have clear referral questions, the clinician can choose test batteries that answer the questions, although it is ultimately it's up to the examiner. Here are some sample referral questions to choose from. The following questions are not exhaustive, they are just a good start.

SAMPLE REFERRAL QUESTIONS

Describe this child's profile of intellectual abilities.

Does this child show academic progress commensurate with his intellectual abilities?

What is the quality of this child's executive functions?

What strengths and weaknesses are noted in this child's executive functions?

Is the child's thinking flexible or rigid?

Describe this child's inhibitory skills.

Is there evidence to support a diagnosis of ADHD?

Is there evidence to support a diagnosis of Dyslexia?

Is there evidence to support a placement for gifted services?

Is additional testing/assessment needed? Why?

What are recommendations for intervention?

WHAT DO WE DO WITH THE DATA?

Clinicians, teachers, school IEP teams, and parents can utilize the neuro-cognitive data to make appropriate referrals, track growth/progress and plan quarterly for the next step of needed interventions. Baseline data is also used to make decisions about what other forms of interventions might be needed. As an example, if the school has conducted an initial classroom observation and noticed that your child is easily distracted and having difficulty completing tests on time, the school might make accommodations to help your child. If the accommodations do not show improvement a referral to a board certified child neuropsychologist or pediatrician may be the next step.

WHAT ARE EXECUTIVE FUNCTIONS?

The term "executive functions" is often heard in clinical offices and school study team meetings. Understanding the quality of a child's executive functions goes beyond an IQ score. For parents, teachers, and clinicians who wish to understand what executive functions are and why they are important, here's the scoop.

Executive function is an umbrella term for the neurologically-based goal-directed skills involving mental control/thinking and self-regulation. The executive functions are a set of brain-based processes that assist us in managing ourselves in daily life. When a child, adolescent, or adult has challenges in any domain of executive function, their overall development, learning, communication, social skills and behavior can be affected.

If you're hearing professionals talk about executive functions they may be referring to:

Your child's ability to pay attention, focus on relevant content, and refrain from being distracted.

Your child's ability to be flexible in his thinking.

Your child's ability to hold information in his short-term or long-term memory. To access, manipulate, apply and utilize that information in real life.

Your child's ability manage his emotions.

Your child's ability to resist being impulsive in his words, thoughts or actions.

Your child's ability to problem solve and make decisions.

Your child's ability to organize, plan, and manage his time, materials and actions.

Your child's ability to plan, pace, maintain and stop his cognitive and motor activities during inappropriate moments.

WHAT DOES THIS HAVE TO DO WITH MISBEHAVIOR?

Sometimes defiance, impulsivity, obsessions, inattention, hyper-focus, cognitive inflexibility and more can look like willful non-compliance. But when we dig deeper, it's not a matter of willfulness, it's biology. This may include deficits in executive functions, deficient neurotransmitters, poor nutrient absorption, sensory overwhelm, language deficits, or difficulty hearing, listening, and understanding.

WHAT YOU CAN **SAY**

It was a rough day for you. I'm going to be your best helper figuring out what went wrong.

It takes time to learn the right thing to do. I'm going to help you.

What do you think gets you in trouble?

What do you think need(s) to change in school for you to be happier?

I'm not mad at you. It's my job to help you.

Instead of talking about consequences, let's talk about what happened today.

You are a loving child and I simply adore you.

Together, we're going to learn what skills you need to feel better in school.

Let's draw a picture about how you well your day will go in school tomorrow.

You will get another chance to try it again tomorrow. I know you can do it!

WHAT YOU CAN **THINK**

It's time for me to be a detective and figure out what is underneath my child's behavior.

I need to consider what is causing my child such difficulty.

I need to talk with the teacher and get her input.

My child is misbehaving for a reason. My job is to figure it out.

I am not going to let negative thoughts about my child's behavior overwhelm me.

Sometimes things are not as they appear on the surface.

The teacher and I need to work together to discover what my child needs that he is not getting.

This is not my child's fault.

My child wants help to behave better.

I will be open to my child getting professional help.

I will learn more about attention and learning issues knowing there is a reason my child behaves as he does.

I will talk with our doctor and consider a professional referral. Maybe we need to have a professional assessment to decide what to do.

I am my child's best advocate, which means I must take the time to study the issues underlying my son's challenges.

WHAT YOU CAN **DO**

Despite your sadness, fears or frustration stay connected and present with your child.

Know that the meaningful moments you share with your child are part of the solution.

Advocate for your child from a place of calm not anger.

Become educated by reading and researching your child's dilemma.

Contact your medical health care provider for referrals for assessment and intervention.

Try to remember that what appears to be willful misbehavior is usually a skill deficit or difficulty modulating emotion.

Work with the school, your child's teacher, or a school advocate to get what your child needs in the classroom.

Bring solutions to the table when you meet with the teacher.

Share your BLOOM book with educators. Help them understand the approach you are taking and what works for your child.

Here are some helpful resources to understand the landscape of challenges we often see in children at home and in school.

» Arrowsmith-Young, Barbara (2012). The Woman Who Changed Her Brain: And Other Inspiring Stories of Pioneering Brain Transformation.

» Barkley, Russell (2012). Executive Functions: What They Are, How They Work, and Why They Evolved.

» Bialer, Doreit & Miller, Lucy Jane (2011). No Longer A SECRET: Unique Common Sense Strategies for Children with Sensory or Motor Challenges.

» Biel, Lindsay and Peske, Nancy (2009). Raising a Sensory Smart Child: The Definitive Handbook for Helping Your Child with Sensory Processing Issues.

» Brown, Peter C. et al. (2014). Make It Stick.

» Buzan, T., & Buzan, B. (2010). The Mind Map Book: Unlock Your Creativity, Boost Your Memory, Change Your Life.

» Campbell, Don & Doman, Alex (2012). Healing at the Speed of Sound: How What We Hear Transforms Our Brains and Our Lives.

» Das, J.P & Naglieri, Jack (1994). Assessment of Cognitive Processes: The PASS Theory of Intelligence.

» Dawson, Peg (2009). Smart but Scattered: The Revolutionary "Executive Skills" Approach to Helping Kids Reach Their Potential.

» Dawson, Peg (2010). Executive Skills in Children and Adolescents, Second Edition: A Practical Guide to Assessment and Intervention.

» Eaton, Howard (2010). Brain School.

» Eide, Brock & Eide Fernette (2012). The Dyslexic Advantage: Unlocking the Hidden Potential of the Dyslexic Brain.

» Greene, Ross (2010). The Explosive Child: A New Approach for Understanding and Parenting Easily Frustrated, Chronically Inflexible Children.

» Ito, Masao (2011). The Cerebellum: Brain for an Implicit Self.

» Jensen, Eric (2005). Teaching with the Brain in Mind.

» Koziol, Leonard (2014). The Myth of Executive Functioning: Missing Elements in Conceptualization, Evaluation, and Assessment.

» Koziol, Leonard & Budding, Deborah (2008). Subcortical Structures and Cognition: Implications for Neuropsychological Assessment.

» Malchiodi, Cathy (ED) (2014). Creative Interventions with Traumatized Children.

» Medina, John (2009). Brain Rules: 12 Principles for Surviving and Thriving at Work, Home, and School.

» Meltzer, Lynn (2010). Promoting Executive Function in the Classroom.

» Reno, Tosca (2011). Just The Rules: How to Eat Right.

» Siegel, Dan & Bryson, Payne Tina (2014). No Drama Discipline: The Whole-Brain Way to Calm the Chaos and Nurture Your Child's Developing Mind.

» Siegel, Dan & Bryson, Payne Tina (2012). The Whole Brain Child.

» Webb, James et al (2005). Misdiagnosis and Dual Diagnosis of Gifted Children and Adults.

More tips from Wendy: Five Ways to Keep Your Child in Class and Out of the Principal's Office

SAY

It was a rough day for you. I'm going to be your best helper figuring out what went wrong.

BLOOM 50 Things To Say, Think, And Do With Anxious, Angry, and Over-the-Top Kids

SAY

It takes time to learn the right thing to do. I'm going to help you.

BLOOM 50 Things To Say, Think, And Do With Anxious, Angry, and Over-the-Top Kids

SAY

What do you think gets you in trouble?

BLOOM 50 Things To Say, Think, And Do With Anxious, Angry, and Over-the-Top Kids

SAY

What do you think need(s) to change in school for you to be happier?

BLOOM 50 Things To Say, Think, And Do With Anxious, Angry, and Over-the-Top Kids

SAY

I'm not mad at you. It's my job to help you.

BLOOM 50 Things To Say, Think, And Do With Anxious, Angry, and Over-the-Top Kids

SAY

Instead of talking about consequences, let's talk about what happened today.

BLOOM 50 Things To Say, Think, And Do With Anxious, Angry, and Over-the-Top Kids

SAY

You are a
loving child and
I simply adore
you.

SAY

Together, we're
going to learn
what skills
you need to
feel better
in school.

SAY

Let's draw a
picture about
how you well
your day will
go in school
tomorrow.

SAY

You will get
another chance
to try it again
tomorrow.
I know you can
do it!

SAY

SAY

THINK

It's time for me to be a detective and figure out what is underneath my child's behavior.

BLOOM 50 Things To Say, Think, And Do With Anxious, Angry, and Over-the-Top Kids

THINK

I need to consider what is causing my child such difficulty.

BLOOM 50 Things To Say, Think, And Do With Anxious, Angry, and Over-the-Top Kids

THINK

I need to talk with the teacher and get her input.

BLOOM 50 Things To Say, Think, And Do With Anxious, Angry, and Over-the-Top Kids

THINK

My child is misbehaving for a reason. My job is to figure it out.

BLOOM 50 Things To Say, Think, And Do With Anxious, Angry, and Over-the-Top Kids

THINK

I am not going to let negative thoughts about my child's behavior overwhelm me.

BLOOM 50 Things To Say, Think, And Do With Anxious, Angry, and Over-the-Top Kids

THINK

Sometimes things are not as they appear on the surface.

BLOOM 50 Things To Say, Think, And Do With Anxious, Angry, and Over-the-Top Kids

THINK

The teacher and I need to work together to discover what my child needs that he is not getting.

BLOOM 50 Things To Say, Think, And Do With Anxious, Angry, and Over-the-Top Kids

THINK

This is not my child's fault.

My child wants help to behave better.

BLOOM 50 Things To Say, Think, And Do With Anxious, Angry, and Over-the-Top Kids

THINK

I will be open to my child getting professional help.

BLOOM 50 Things To Say, Think, And Do With Anxious, Angry, and Over-the-Top Kids

THINK

I will learn more about attention and learning issues knowing there is a reason my child behaves as he does.

BLOOM 50 Things To Say, Think, And Do With Anxious, Angry, and Over-the-Top Kids

THINK

I will talk with our doctor and consider a professional referral. Maybe we need to have a professional assessment to decide what to do.

BLOOM 50 Things To Say, Think, And Do With Anxious, Angry, and Over-the-Top Kids

THINK

I am my child's best advocate, which means I must take the time to study the issues underlying my son's challenges.

BLOOM 50 Things To Say, Think, And Do With Anxious, Angry, and Over-the-Top Kids

DO

Despite your sadness, fears or frustration stay connected and present with your child.

BLOOM 50 Things To Say, Think, And Do With Anxious, Angry, and Over-the-Top Kids

DO

Know that the meaningful moments you share with your child are part of the solution.

BLOOM 50 Things To Say, Think, And Do With Anxious, Angry, and Over-the-Top Kids

DO

Advocate for your child from a place of calm not anger.

BLOOM 50 Things To Say, Think, And Do With Anxious, Angry, and Over-the-Top Kids

DO

Become educated by reading and researching your child's dilemma.

BLOOM 50 Things To Say, Think, And Do With Anxious, Angry, and Over-the-Top Kids

DO

Contact your medical health care provider for referrals for assessment and intervention.

BLOOM 50 Things To Say, Think, And Do With Anxious, Angry, and Over-the-Top Kids

DO

Try to remember that what appears to be willful misbehavior is usually a skill deficit or difficulty modulating emotion.

BLOOM 50 Things To Say, Think, And Do With Anxious, Angry, and Over-the-Top Kids

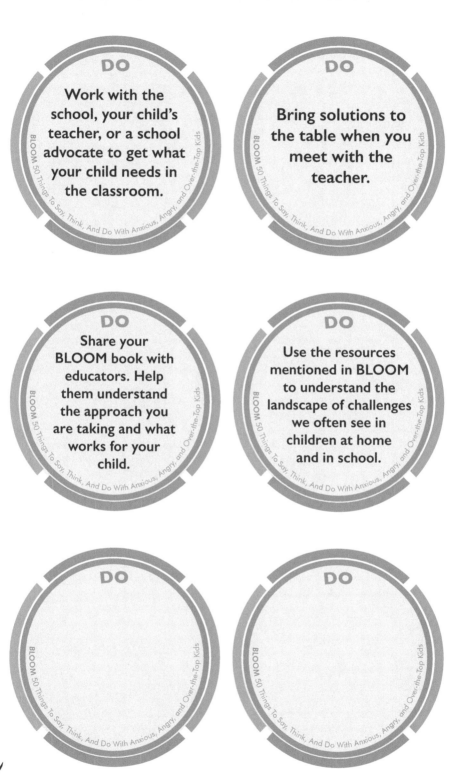

DO

Work with the school, your child's teacher, or a school advocate to get what your child needs in the classroom.

BLOOM 50 Things To Say, Think, And Do With Anxious, Angry, and Over-the-Top Kids

DO

Bring solutions to the table when you meet with the teacher.

BLOOM 50 Things To Say, Think, And Do With Anxious, Angry, and Over-the-Top Kids

DO

Share your BLOOM book with educators. Help them understand the approach you are taking and what works for your child.

BLOOM 50 Things To Say, Think, And Do With Anxious, Angry, and Over-the-Top Kids

DO

Use the resources mentioned in BLOOM to understand the landscape of challenges we often see in children at home and in school.

BLOOM 50 Things To Say, Think, And Do With Anxious, Angry, and Over-the-Top Kids

DO

BLOOM 50 Things To Say, Think, And Do With Anxious, Angry, and Over-the-Top Kids

DO

BLOOM 50 Things To Say, Think, And Do With Anxious, Angry, and Over-the-Top Kids

CHAPTER 9

Tearful Goodbyes

SMOOTHER SEPARATIONS

"My four-year-old daughter cries every day when I drop her off at preschool. She has been home with me up until this point. She clings to my leg making it difficult for me to get out the door. It breaks my heart to leave while she is in tears every day. Is this separation anxiety? What should I do? Should I take her out of the program and just let her stay home with me?"

WHAT'S THE DEAL BEHIND SEPARATION ANXIETY?

Trouble separating is based in human biology. Children are bonded to their parents for a reason. Keeping close proximity to a parental figure ensures survival. Children feel safe and protected with their parent. From a developmental perspective and survival stance, human beings are hard wired to seek safety, security and comfort. It assists with our longevity as a species. Individually, it allows us to master our environments. No wonder kids want to be with their parents.

IS SEPARATION ANXIETY NORMAL? WHO GETS IT?

Anxiety disorders including separation anxiety are caused by an interplay of genetics, biology and environmental factors. For some children, separation anxiety is a normal phenomenon that generally ends during the toddler phase. But anxiety can also be present for older children (preschool and kindergarten age) who are experiencing first-time separations from caregivers. Some children are more sensitive to separations than others.

Separation anxiety might also signal a brain uniqueness. Recently, researchers imaged the brains of children with and without preschool anxiety disorders. They found that in those children who had an anxiety disorder, the prefrontal cortex and the amygdala, talked to each other less. This weaker functional connectivity may be at the root of some forms of anxiety. Using the Bloom neuro-cognitive strategies may help enhance brain connectivity through repetition of language and actions that enhance a sense of emotional safety.

WHAT'S GOING ON BEHIND THE TEARS AND THE TANTRUMS?

Your child's system is in a state of alarm. When stressed, her body produces the hormone cortisol, which floods her system. This puts her in the fight, flight or freeze mode. Feeling out of sorts, her first inclination is to cling to you, to cry and to try to avoid the separation. It is likely your child misses you when you are apart. Her heart wants to be with you, but the reality is that this cannot always be the case. She is sad and may feel overwhelmed with emotion. Some children, particularly those with intense temperaments or anxiety, have strong reactions to separations.

WHAT'S THE DEAL WITH ANXIETY AND CAN KIDS REALLY HAVE IT?

Anxiety isn't one size fits all. It comes in many shapes and sizes and can range from mild to debilitating. Childhood anxiety is real and it can present itself as fearfulness, but it can also present itself as defiance, anger and explosiveness. That may be surprising to many parents. Some parents bring their kids to therapy because of the difficulty they have managing their child's apparent willful non-compliance, such as ongoing explosions and irritability, only to find that when the anxiety was identified and treated, their child was much more at ease and compliant.

HOW LONG WILL THIS LAST?

While separation anxiety is something many kids go through, it is usually a transient situation. Most children will learn to cope and will allow trusted others to care for them. When anxiety is protracted, and continues on for a length of time, your child may benefit from extra assistance in learning how to manage it. This will go a long way towards helping your child feel more secure and successful.

WHAT CAN HELP?

If needed, ask your pediatrician for a referral to a good therapist or counselor with experience in this area. There are some self-help resources available, but we urge you get professional assistance to help your child in an effective and expedient manner.

A book we really love is **Worried No More**, by Aureen Pinto Wagner. This resource will help parents, teachers, and counselors better understand anxiety, as well as helping kids cope. Another workbook for you is **The Relaxation and Stress Reduction Workbook for Kids: Help for Children to Cope with Stress, Anxiety, and Transitions** by Laurence Shapiro et al.

For books you can read to your children, try **When I Miss You** by Cornelia Maude Spelman, **The Invisible String** by Patrice Karst, **I Love You All Day Long** by Francesca Rusackas, **Llama Llama Misses Mama** by Anna Dewdney and **The Kissing Hand** by Audrey Penn.

MY HUSBAND THINKS OUR CHILD IS TRYING TO MANIPULATE US COULD THIS BE WHAT'S REALLY GOING ON?

Children who are having trouble separating are not trying to manipulate you, ruin your day, or make you late for work. They are trying their best to become independent but need your help, as well as the help of their caregivers. Your child is afraid and wants to know she is safe and that you are doing what is good for her.

WHAT CAN THE PRESCHOOL TEACHER DO TO HELP?

Quality caregivers and educators understand this difficult transition and are fairly well-versed on assisting your child. Empathizing with your child's feelings and supporting her in dealing with her feelings will help her move through this transition more quickly. Teachers can also help your child by giving her a role in the classroom such as door holder or snack server to help her engage in the classroom. A great research-supported method for engagement is to allow the anxious child to teach something she knows well to the class, this is a real confidence booster.

THIS SEPARATION IS REALLY HARD FOR ME, TOO. COULD MY CHILD BE AWARE OF THAT? MIGHT THAT FEED HER ANXIETY?

Children can sense if you are feeling uncertain, upset or having trouble separating yourself. In some cases, the child is expressing what the parent is feeling. How do you feel about separating from your child? It's okay to feel sad when your child first enters school. If you can find a way to metabolize your own feelings your child will find it easier to separate as well.

Here's a craft you can do with your child, to help her remember you are in each other's hearts, even when apart.

A CRAFTY WAY TO DEAL WITH SEPARATION ANXIETY

Using different colors of construction paper, cut out one large and one small heart from each color. Glue the smaller heart of opposite color on top of the larger heart. The outside heart will represent your child's heart and the inside heart will represent yours, being a tangible reminder that you are always in your child's heart. Now, repeat the process and make a heart for yourself, with the smaller heart representing your child being always in your heart when you are away from each other. Let her keep her hearts in her backpack and you can keep yours in your briefcase or tote.

WHAT YOU CAN **SAY**

It can be sad to be apart, but our sads can become glads.

I used to feel sad when my mom left me, too. Then I made friends and started to like school. What do you think will help you feel better at school?

When Mommy goes grocery shopping, we are apart. But then we come back together.

Daddy doesn't cry when he leaves for work in the morning because he knows he will be back for dinner. He probably cried too when he was little, but then he learned we always come back together.

When we say goodbye, hello is right around the corner.

It's okay to cry when you are sad. Crying lets you work through your feelings.

When you are done crying, what would you like to do first at school?

I will see you right after your outside playtime is done.

We will talk about our rainbows and hurricanes when I pick you up. (Our rainbows are the bright spots in our day, while the hurricanes are the low spots.)

I'll put a butterfly sticker on this little piece of paper. You can keep it in your pocket all day and touch it when you miss me.

Let's play the 'Hello Game'! I'll say 'hello' and you tell me one thing that made you smile today.

It can feel good to hold your teacher's hand for a moment when you feel sad.

You can think of things that make you laugh when you are feeling sad. Like when our kitty slept on Daddy's head.

You can think of a favorite memory of the two of us together to lift up your happy heart.

I see that it's hard for you to put your worried feelings into words. Let me help you find the words.

One day, you won't feel so upset when I leave. Watch and see!

We will get through this together.

WHAT YOU CAN **THINK**

Separation anxiety can be a common experience for many young children.

My child feels most safe with me. I will help her feel safe with teachers and friends.

As my child engages more in school, she will feel better.

Art is known to increase the creative centers in the brain, I will draw with my daughter to explore her experiences, this will help her look at her feelings in a new way.

I'll help my child find soothing activities she can do in school to feel better in class, like drawing or crafts.

I'll help my child connect more with her teacher so they enjoys being with the teacher during the day.

I'll make a bridge between home and school by helping my child bring something from home, like a cherished toy to share with her teacher.

I will show her through my words, actions and beliefs that she is safe at preschool and that I trust she is in good hands.

My child is ready for school. I am doing the right thing.

I will be trustworthy by always being on time when school gets out.

I will take my child's feelings seriously and not dismiss them.

WHAT YOU CAN **DO**

Role-play going to school when at home. Show your child what she can enjoy in school.

Preview her day as you head off to school. Talk about who will be there and what they will do together.

Know that separating will get easier.

Calm your own feelings and even tears, your child will sense when you feel secure leaving her at school.

Allow her to cry and provide empathy, but also help her plan for transitioning into fun activities at school.

Be reliable and consistent when you drop your child off and pick her up.

Know that as she becomes more connected at school your child will enjoy school more.

Think about the match between your child and the school, is the school meeting her needs?

Talk with a trusted friend about your own feelings.

Validate your child's feelings. Make all feelings okay!

IN A NUTSHELL: WHY IS SEPARATING SO DIFFICULT FOR SOME CHILDREN?

1. Children are biologically wired to want to be near you.

2. Their feelings are bigger than they are.

3. They do not have the skills to cope with overwhelming feelings and need your help.

4. They may have fears about their safety and security, yet cannot put those fears into words.

5. They may sense your uncertainty about separating and wonder if it is okay.

6. New situations can cause anxiety.

7. The fear of the unknown may be most difficult. Once children settle into the new routine, the intensity of separating diminishes.

8. Young children have no concept of time.

9. They are nervous and uptight but have no words to express it.

WHEN IT'S HARD FOR YOU TO LEAVE

Leaving a crying child at preschool (or daycare) is unsettling for most parents. Our natural instinct is to sooth and assist our child, and it is difficult to see them so upset. What can be even more troubling is having to leave before our child calms down. It may help to know that your child's independence grows when she can be soothed by other caring adults. As she begins to rely on other trusted adults to help her calm down, her world expands. That's important to her growth.

SHE JUST WON'T STOP CRYING. NOW WHAT?

Your child's world may seem turned upside down. It is tough to be away from a loved grown-up. She may whine, cry or cling in protest of you leaving. Providing her with a "transitional object" (stuffed animal or other sentimental item), that she can keep in her backpack or cubby may help ease the separation. When your child senses that "all is okay" with her new environment, adult caregiver, and routine, she will be able to transition easier. When you handle this in a calm, matter-of-fact, yet nurturing way, you send your child a strong signal that she can relax and enjoy their new surroundings.

A FEW CLOSING WORDS...

You've been helping your child learn how to cope with lots of feelings of upset since she was born. You've helped her through hunger pangs, wet diapers, scary noises, strange adults and even boredom. You've given her coping skills, which all help her on her way to independence. This is another step in that process. Learning how to separate is a universal experience of all children and parents. Know you are not alone!

More tips from Wendy: Five Little Known
Tricks to Ease Seperation Anxiety

SAY

It can be sad to be apart, but our sads can become glads.

BLOOM 50 Things To Say, Think, And Do With Anxious, Angry, and Over-the-Top Kids

SAY

I used to feel sad when my mom left me, too. Then I made friends and started to like school. What do you think will help you feel better at school?

BLOOM 50 Things To Say, Think, And Do With Anxious, Angry, and Over-the-Top Kids

SAY

When Mommy goes grocery shopping, we are apart. But then we come back together.

BLOOM 50 Things To Say, Think, And Do With Anxious, Angry, and Over-the-Top Kids

SAY

Daddy doesn't cry when he leaves for work because he knows he will be back for dinner. He probably cried too when he was little, but then he learned we always come back together.

BLOOM 50 Things To Say, Think, And Do With Anxious, Angry, and Over-the-Top Kids

SAY

When we say goodbye, hello is right around the corner.

BLOOM 50 Things To Say, Think, And Do With Anxious, Angry, and Over-the-Top Kids

SAY

It's okay to cry when you are sad. Crying lets you work through your feelings.

BLOOM 50 Things To Say, Think, And Do With Anxious, Angry, and Over-the-Top Kids

SAY

When you are done crying, what would you like to do first at school?

BLOOM 50 Things To Say, Think, And Do With Anxious, Angry, and Over-the-Top Kids

SAY

I will see you right after your outside playtime is done.

BLOOM 50 Things To Say, Think, And Do With Anxious, Angry, and Over-the-Top Kids

SAY

We will talk about our rainbows and hurricanes when I pick you up.

BLOOM 50 Things To Say, Think, And Do With Anxious, Angry, and Over-the-Top Kids

SAY

I'll put a butterfly sticker on this little piece of paper. You can keep it in your pocket all day and touch it when you miss me.

BLOOM 50 Things To Say, Think, And Do With Anxious, Angry, and Over-the-Top Kids

SAY

Let's play the 'Hello Game'! I'll say 'hello' and you tell me one thing that made you smile today.

BLOOM 50 Things To Say, Think, And Do With Anxious, Angry, and Over-the-Top Kids

SAY

It can feel good to hold your teacher's hand for a moment when you feel sad.

BLOOM 50 Things To Say, Think, And Do With Anxious, Angry, and Over-the-Top Kids

SAY

You can think of things that make you laugh when you are feeling sad. Like when our kitty slept on Daddy's head.

SAY

You can think of a favorite memory of the two of us together to lift up your happy heart.

SAY

I see that it's hard for you to put your worried feelings into words. Let me help you find the words.

SAY

One day, you won't feel so upset when I leave. Watch and see!

SAY

SAY

THINK

Separation anxiety can be a common experience for many young children.

BLOOM 50 Things To Say, Think, And Do With Anxious, Angry, and Over-the-Top Kids

THINK

My child feels most safe with me. I will help her feel safe with teachers and friends.

BLOOM 50 Things To Say, Think, And Do With Anxious, Angry, and Over-the-Top Kids

THINK

As my child engages more in school, she will feel better.

BLOOM 50 Things To Say, Think, And Do With Anxious, Angry, and Over-the-Top Kids

THINK

Art is known to increase the creative centers in the brain, I will draw with my daughter to explore her experiences, this will help her look at her feelings in a new way.

BLOOM 50 Things To Say, Think, And Do With Anxious, Angry, and Over-the-Top Kids

THINK

I'll help my child find soothing activities she can do in school to feel better in class, like drawing or crafts.

BLOOM 50 Things To Say, Think, And Do With Anxious, Angry, and Over-the-Top Kids

THINK

I'll help my child connect more with her teacher so they enjoy being with the teacher during the day.

BLOOM 50 Things To Say, Think, And Do With Anxious, Angry, and Over-the-Top Kids

THINK

I'll make a bridge between home and school by helping my child bring something from home, like a cherished toy to share with her teacher.

BLOOM 50 Things To Say, Think, And Do With Anxious, Angry, and Over-the-Top Kids

THINK

I will show her through my words, actions and beliefs that she is safe at preschool and that I trust she is in good hands.

BLOOM 50 Things To Say, Think, And Do With Anxious, Angry, and Over-the-Top Kids

THINK

My child is ready for school. I am doing the right thing.

BLOOM 50 Things To Say, Think, And Do With Anxious, Angry, and Over-the-Top Kids

THINK

I will be trustworthy by always being on time when school gets out.

BLOOM 50 Things To Say, Think, And Do With Anxious, Angry, and Over-the-Top Kids

THINK

I will take my child's feelings seriously and not dismiss them.

BLOOM 50 Things To Say, Think, And Do With Anxious, Angry, and Over-the-Top Kids

DO

Role-play going to school when at home. Show your child what she can enjoy in school.

BLOOM 50 Things To Say, Think, And Do With Anxious, Angry, and Over-the-Top Kids

DO

Preview her day as you head off to school. Talk about who will be there and what they will do together.

BLOOM 50 Things To Say, Think, And Do With Anxious, Angry, and Over-the-Top Kids

DO

Know that separating will get easier.

BLOOM 50 Things To Say, Think, And Do With Anxious, Angry, and Over-the-Top Kids

DO

Calm your own feelings and even tears, your child will sense when you feel secure leaving her at school.

BLOOM 50 Things To Say, Think, And Do With Anxious, Angry, and Over-the-Top Kids

DO

Allow her to cry and provide empathy, but also help her plan for transitioning into fun activities at school.

BLOOM 50 Things To Say, Think, And Do With Anxious, Angry, and Over-the-Top Kids

DO

Be reliable and consistent when you drop your child off and pick her up.

BLOOM 50 Things To Say, Think, And Do With Anxious, Angry, and Over-the-Top Kids

DO

Know that as she becomes more connected at school your child will enjoy school more.

DO

Think about the match between your child and the school, is the school meeting her needs?

DO

Talk with a trusted friend about your own feelings.

DO

Validate your child's feelings. Make all feelings okay!

DO

DO

CHAPTER 10

Trauma

TRAUMA: WHEN PAIN DRIVES BEHAVIOR

> "There are wounds that never show on the body that are
> deeper and more hurtful than anything that bleeds."
> ~ Laurell K. Hamilton

I t can be said that behavior is driven by unseen forces. Never is this truer than when trauma is involved. These unseen forces, be they neurological, biological or psychological, kick into overdrive when trauma is part of the equation.

The following stories may seem unrelated at first glance, but they all have a common thread: Trauma. The three distinct stories that follow come from three different families from across the globe.

"Why does Joey 'zone out' so much during school? I've just returned from his parent-teacher conference and his teacher believes he is bright and capable of much more than is demonstrating in the classroom. More than that, he sometimes lashes out at other kids and adults for no apparent reason. I just don't get it. Life was rough for us, and he saw a lot more troublesome things than he should have in his younger years, but that ended a few years ago, when my ex and I split up. Our home is now calm and relaxed; it's just Joey and me. Why is he still struggling? Shouldn't he be moving on already?"

More discussion with Joey's mom uncovers that he was exposed to violence even prior to his birth. Joey's biological father was abusive to Joey's mom during her pregnancy and for Joey's first five years of life until they split up. Though Joey never experienced physical abuse by his father once he was born, he did hear and witness multiple incidences of violence towards his mother throughout his young life.

In a different story, but one not altogether different, we hear from another set of parents:

"Ailene was a happy-go-lucky preschooler until our family experienced a house fire. We are grateful that our entire family and pets were able to escape unharmed, but we lost everything in the blaze. Ailene is afraid to go to preschool, won't sleep in her new room at night, cries at the drop of a hat and is very difficult to comfort when she is upset. This has been going on for months."

And finally, one more plea for help from yet another family. Trevas' mom tells the story in her own words:

"Trevas was a healthy toddler until a car accident in which his father was severely injured. Trevas and his father were both taken by separate ambulances to the hospital, which is where I met up with them. Trevas was medically cleared and released to me. Because his dad was badly injured, I needed to stay with him. My parents, whom Trevas knows well, came to pick him up. Now, 6 months after the accident, Trevas' dad is doing much better and is back to work. Trevas, in the meantime, is still having nightmares, cries when he is put into his car seat, at times, and has taken to "rocking" when he is upset. On really bad days, he bangs his head against the wall. We are so worried about him."

All of these children's behavioral manifestations are likely a direct reaction to trauma they've experienced in their lives. We've heard countless stories like these from parents and caregivers.

HELP ME UNDERSTAND THESE BEHAVIORS

From a brain-based perspective, traumatized children may react to seemingly inert situations with strong, socially unacceptable responses. Rather than thinking these children are engaging in maladaptive behaviors, we must honor they are in survival mode and doing the very best they can at the time. They are responding to real or perceived threats and these behaviors are functional for them in some way. This explains the behavior that occurs in traumatized children that appears irrational to others.

In children with no trauma, all parts of the brain work in concert to decide how to solve the problem at hand. In difficult times, most trauma-free children can think things through, problem-solve, and analyze their situation while simultaneously being aware of their sense of self and their emotions.

Meanwhile, traumatized children downshift into the lower parts of their brain. Their analytical abilities are suppressed and the emotional brain kicks into high gear. They are operating from their limbic system and are focused on survival. This can cause over-the-top reactions, caused by an uncontrolled sense of helplessness and rage. Alternatively, the child may freeze up or flee to avoid the situation altogether. Some children literally seek refuge under a table, desk or a bed.

When a traumatized child is responding from their limbic brain, their capacity to problem solve and self-soothe are diminished. Their reactions may cause them to act out in ways that seem completely unrelated to the situation at hand. These reactions are not very well-received during birthday parties with peers, while in the classroom, or on the playground. In fact, these behaviors often land traumatized kids in a world of trouble with parents, teachers, and other adult caregivers.

WHAT ARE SOME SPECIFIC CAUSES OF TRAUMA?

Trauma can have its origins in any number of situations or experiences. According to the **National Child Traumatic Stress Network (NCTSN),** there are multiple sources of trauma for children, including, but not limited to:

- » Community Violence
- » Complex Trauma
- » Domestic Violence
- » Early Childhood Trauma
- » Medical Trauma
- » Natural Disasters
- » Neglect
- » Physical Abuse
- » Refugee and War Zone Trauma
- » School Violence
- » Sexual Abuse
- » Terrorism
- » Traumatic Grief

BRAVE WARRIORS

This chapter is dedicated to these children, brave warriors, who despite difficult circumstances, continue to move forward. We hope to help you understand that trauma can contribute to behavioral issues long after the traumatic event took place. These behaviors may crop up at unexpected times and seem out of context to you. That is the nature of trauma.

When a child has been exposed to multiple traumas over time, it can have an exponential effect. The impact is cumulative. The attack from the trauma on the child's psychological, emotional and physiological states requires ongoing opportunities to self-regulate. In short, the child will continue to experience over-the-top states of arousal, until he can be successful at managing them. This will necessitate much patience and understanding on the part of the adult caregiver.

CAN I HELP MY CHILD THROUGH THIS ALONE?

There are many things you can do to support your child through trauma. In addition, we highly recommend that you seek professional care when a child has been traumatized. A trauma-trained professional will address the complex needs of a traumatized child, by bearing witness to the trauma and offering activities that will help the child process the events so that it minimizes its impact on the child's daily functioning.

AN EMERGENCY FOR THE BODY, MIND, AND EMOTIONS

If your child were having a medical emergency, you would take them to the nearest emergency department at the closest hospital. You would offer emotional support and care while trained doctors attended to their medical condition. Trauma can be thought of as an emergency for the body, mind, and emotions as trauma reactions include physiological, cognitive, and affective components. These trauma reactions are **not** short-lived.

Trauma causes ongoing reactions that require continuing intervention. Managing the terror, anxiety, as well as the physiological, behavioral and emotional fallout of trauma can be a challenge. Having a trained professional can ease this process and help restore equilibrium more quickly and more efficiently than if a child is left to deal with the trauma alone. We'll give you resources at the end of this chapter to help find a qualified and licensed expert in this field.

HOW LONG WILL THE TRAUMA LAST?

There is no timetable when it comes to healing trauma. Each child's journey to healing will be unique. We know the impact of trauma can have a marked and lasting effect on behavior. Trauma changes everything. The actual symptoms of trauma, and their duration are determined by a number of things including:

- » The severity of the event
- » The duration of the trauma
- » The amount of destruction witnessed or experienced
- » Caregiver reactions
- » Compounded trauma (if the child has been exposed to multiple traumatic situations)
- » The level of family and community support.

Individual personality and resiliency characteristics, as well as the age of the child at the time the trauma occurred, will also factor in when determining how long the trauma will impact any given child. A child cannot just "get over" trauma. Learning how to manage the emotional and physiological symptoms of trauma is a process.

WHY DO TRAUMATIZED KIDS DO WHAT THEY DO?

Trauma can change both the structure and function of the brain. Medical imaging can show the damage done to brains by trauma. It can also show the repair of these areas when interventions to treat trauma are successful. When one understands trauma and how it impacts the brain and behavior, it becomes much easier to understand some of the baffling and seemingly irrational actions that occur in children who have experienced trauma.

When we deal with children from a trauma-informed perspective, we are able to move away from asking, "What's WRONG with you?" and move toward asking, "What HAPPENED to you?"

SHOULDN'T ALL MISBEHAVIOR BE TREATED THE SAME WAY?

We as a society have been stuck for a long time treating trauma reactions as if they are misbehaviors. Using traditional approaches such as ignoring, walking away, and utilizing distraction does nothing to discharge the trauma, nor does it teach more adaptive behaviors.

Doling out consequences doesn't help, either. This is because everything we have done traditionally to try to change behavior is top down. Conventional discipline appeals to the cognitive part of the brain. This is not where trauma lives. Trauma lives is in the non-verbal parts of the brain, where words mean little. In short, when you try to appeal to a child's senses, the trauma cannot hear what you are saying.

> Conventional discipline appeals to the cognitive part of the brain. This is not where trauma lives. Traditional discipline will do nothing to change behavior that is driven by trauma.

TRAUMA REQUIRES SOMETHING DIFFERENT

When a child has experienced trauma, it's almost as if a whole new set of parenting and teaching rules have to be put into place. The child's behavior has to be looked at through the lens of trauma. Understanding how trauma affects mood and behavior will go a long way towards reducing the frustration of adult caregivers, and allow them to better approach the child from an informed perspective that helps soothe the child's limbic brain, and helps them return from a state of high-alert/high-stress to baseline functioning.

ALL ADULTS HAVE THE CAPACITY TO HELP CHILDREN WITH TRAUMA

Physical and emotional safety is something all children need, but traumatized children need this even more. It's also something all adult caregivers are capable of providing. You needn't have a degree in psychology or traumatology in order to assist a child. If you can learn not to personalize behavior, have ears that can listen, a heart that cares, and can keep calm under fire, you have everything you need to help a child. Like we've mentioned in other sections of this book, managing your own emotional reactions is paramount to helping a child regain a state of equilibrium.

CAN A BRAIN THAT'S BEEN TRAUMATIZED HEAL?

When we know what helps, we can provide a corrective emotional experience to a child who is hurting. The simple antidote to trauma follows: sensitivity, patience, kindness and presence. The aforementioned caregiver qualities can help brains heal from distress and improve trauma-driven behavior. Providing comfort, support and encouragement does not require any special or advanced scientific training. Know that you have the power to help children heal.

THREE STEPS TO MANAGING TRAUMA-DRIVEN BEHAVIOR

The three steps to managing trauma-driven behavior are related to best practices in managing any childhood behavior, and the same approach we advocate throughout BLOOM. In the case of trauma, we are applying these same basic principles, from a trauma-informed perspective. They are as follows:

Don't personalize. Managing your own reaction to the behavior is your first line of defense. Our *"What You Can Think"* section will be of immeasurable help in this regard. A child with a challenging behavior is not out to get you, nor are they trying to make your life miserable. They are trying, the best they can, to cope with an overwhelmingly difficult situation.

Help the child's limbic system calm down. Move away from the focus of "stopping the behavior" immediately, and move towards trying to help the child's limbic system settle down. A gentle, calm approach is in order. Our *"What You Can Say"* section can help get you started. It's important to bear in mind, you are not trying to appeal to the cognitive brain at this point. You are merely using your words as a calming technique. Your tone, pacing and volume of speech should be relaxed. You'll want your words to convey a sense of physical and emotional safety. It's not so much what you say as how you are saying it. There are no perfect words.

Provide a creative outlet. When a child is traumatized, we cannot appeal to his intellect. Therefore, telling him to "calm down" is useless. Because trauma is stored in nonverbal memory, we must appeal to the limbic brain and the sensorimotor system. An activity that engages and soothes the limbic brain, such as drawing, or helps calm the child's bodily sensations of distress, such as a deep-breathing exercise, is your best bet. Be sure to see "What to Do" for several other intervention options.

WHAT YOU CAN **SAY**

This is such a struggle right now for you.

You are having a hard time right now.

Things are upsetting you right now.

You look like you need my help.

I'll stay right by you and help you.

Let's take some deep breaths together.

Would rubbing your back help you calm down?

Would you like to pound some clay until you feel better?

Rocking in the chair can help you feel better. Give it a try.

Want to blow some bubbles to help you calm down?

I'll walk around the block with you, if you'd like.

Let's shoot some hoops until you feel better.

Would like to draw me a picture that shows what's bothering you?

Would you like to draw what your (angry, sad, scared) feeling looks like?

We can just sit here quietly together.

WHAT YOU CAN **THINK**

This is a result of the trauma.

There is nothing wrong with this child. It's what happened to him that's the problem.

This child is not the problem. The problem is the problem.

This is triggering her. She is in a state of hyper-arousal.

This is the child's limbic brain speaking. There is no logical reasoning with it.

This behavior doesn't have to make sense to me.

The child may not be able to verbalize what is bothering her.

This child is reaching out for help.

I'm going to keep myself calm so I can help her be calm.

The first thing I try may not work. I will keep trying until we find a solution that helps.

I can help this child.

My goal is to help her calm down and feel safe.

WHAT YOU CAN **DO**

Stay calm and relaxed. It's the only way you can help the child.

Talk in a low, soothing voice.

Stay by the child, but be sure not to crowd them.

Provide physical outlets for the feeling.

Provide tactile input (if the child can tolerate it and agrees with it), such as gentle massage, "rain" on the back, letters or numbers traced on the child's back.

Provide a rocking chair or rocking horse.

Provide a bean bag to sit in.

Provide headphones that are noise canceling.

Provide chewing gum. Provide play dough or clay.

Provide drawing paper and art supplies.

Provide weighted blankets or weighted stuffed animals.

Enlist the help of a qualified and licensed mental health professional well versed in trauma and young children.

TEACH MINDFULNESS

Teach mindfulness and relaxation. This approach is one of great promise. We use the relaxation exercises (below) in our own practices with children and adolescents. It really helps calm the limbic system and return kids to psychological and physical safety, so they can upshift and use their whole brain. Kids ask to do these exercises, once they get used to using them. The response is incredible. We use both the free resources from Dartmouth College and the wonderful resources from Stress Free Kids on a regular basis. You can find a list of those resources below:

Relaxation: Free MP3 downloads from Dartmouth University

dartmouth.edu/~healthed/relax/downloads.html
StressFreeKids.com
RelaxKids.com

MORE RESOURCES:

Child Trauma Academy
childtrauma.org
The National child Traumatic Stress Network
nctsnet.org
The Center for Trauma and Loss: Parent Resources
starr.org/training/tlc/resources-for-parents

LIMBIC LIMBO: STRATEGIES THAT CAN HELP

Getting around the child's defensive brain, so you can help her calm down.

Adults often feel helpless and hopeless when faced with a child whose trauma has been activated, and who appears to have reached the point of no return. In these moments, it's important to remind ourselves that the child's system is in complete overdrive. The child is likely feeling terrorized. In these moments, we act as external regulators, helping them integrate elements of their thoughts, feelings and bodily sensations.

A promising approach was utilized for a three-month period in one school. Lakes and Hoyt (2004) conducted a study with children in Kindergarten through fifth grade. These children were instructed in martial arts, during which time, they were encouraged to focus on asking themselves three things:

- » Where am I?
- » What am I doing?
- » What should I be doing?

When compared to a control group, the children in Lakes and Hoyt's study had better behavior in the classroom, enhanced socialization and improved performance on a mental math test.

It's exciting to see the changes that take place when we intentionally help kids become more grounded, attend to the here and now and keep them focused on the task at hand. We can see these three questions incorporated into a morning circle routine in early childhood classrooms, and utilized throughout the day when children need to feel more grounded.

MORE HELPING TECHNIQUES

When it comes to trauma, or anything else for that matter, the more tools we have in our toolbox from which to choose in managing it, the better.

Combining techniques to help children whose systems are over-activated, over-aroused and over-the-top makes for much more powerful results. Helping kids get grounded (as mentioned above) is one step. Next, we can introduce some "Balloon Breathing" or "Artful Interventions".

BALLOON BREATHING

Teaching kids to calm down is both a science and an art. When any of us are agitated, upset or anxious, our prefrontal cortexes take a hiatus and we're left to deal with just our emotional brain (which, if you haven't noticed, doesn't always exercise the best judgment or make the best decisions).

It's clear that stress, anxiety, anger issues and other concerns impact our ability to self-regulate (the ability to calm ourselves down and find balance). We can push back, and teach our children to do the same.

WHEN KIDS' ENGINES ARE REVVED UP

When kids' (or our) engines are revved up, a chemical chain reaction of sorts takes place, dumping adrenaline, cortisol and other hormones throughout our body. This served our ancestors well when they stared down the face of a sabre-toothed tiger and needed the energy and stamina to escape their predator. However, it's not such a great thing for a kid when they are being asked to complete a math assignment, get their coat and boots on for recess or get ready for bed. What looks like oppositional behavior may actually be stress and anxiety. But how do we change it?

GETTING TO CALM

In order to get the prefrontal cortex back online, we need to sooth the limbic system (emotional brain). One of the simplest ways to achieve this is by breathing. Here are two quick breathing exercises, one of which can be used anywhere by anyone and they're FREE! The other one can be used by anyone, too, but it requires bubbles (or you can just pretend you're blowing bubbles).

BALLOON BREATHING

When we become stressed, we often breathe very shallow, filling our chests with air. Deep breathing requires that we fill our bellies with our breath. We may actually feel our diaphragm expand and contract when we do it right. For kids, we can tell them to pretend they have a balloon in their belly that is filling with air when they breathe in, and that it deflates when they breathe out. Demonstrate and practice with them, how to take deep breaths and exhale. Encourage kids to hold to their hands on their bellies to feel them expand when they are first learning how to do this. Repeat several times. There you have it, plain and simple... Balloon Breathing.

Calm Down, Kids!

Balloon Bellies & Bubble Breathing

kidlutions.com

BUBBLE BREATHING

This one is great for outdoors or anywhere else if you don't mind if a bit of bubble solution spills over, such as a kitchen or bathroom. For this technique, simply ask kids to inhale deeply (filling their bellies with air) and exhale slowly, blowing the bubbles while they do so. This will help kids become more conscious and intentional about breathing out slowly. (It's pretty hard to blow bubbles when you are breathing forcefully out.) When kids become stressed, they can be encouraged to balloon breathe or bubble breathe (with or without the bubbles).

WHEN/HOW TO TEACH THESE SKILLS

Teach kids these skills when they are relaxed and unhurried. It's of limited use to try to teach such skills when a child is already in overdrive. The brain is not receptive to new learning at this point. A relaxed and happy brain learns best.

Once you have taught this technique, you'll want to continue to review it, so when it is needed in the heat of the moment, your child will recall how to do it.

KEEP REVIEWING!

This isn't a one and done technique. We need to remind kids and practice these techniques with them several times before it becomes something they naturally do on their own. Eventually, they will do it on their own. Isn't it grand? We can teach great coping and self-regulation skills that will last your child her whole life through!

(The above exercise was excerpted and adapted from kidlutions.com)

ARTFUL INTERVENTIONS

We've shared that trauma resides in the nonverbal part of the brain, so how about a little coping tool that provides help from the nonverbal part of the brain, too? Art originates from the nonverbal part of the brain, is pictorial and symbolic. When a child is falling apart at the seams, a helpful way to help bring him back together is to allow him to discharge the feeling. There's often no better way to do this than art. The child can be invited to draw a picture of how he's feeling, how big his scared, mad or upset feeling is and then exert his own sense of control over that feeling by deciding if wants the parent or teacher to hold onto it, if he'd like to rip it into pieces and throw it away, or if he'd like stomp on it until the feeling subsides. This way of responding may take less than five minutes, all told, yet has engaged the child's nonverbal brain, provided a repetitive and soothing limbic activity (painting or coloring or drawing), as well as a physical outlet (ripping, stomping, throwing).

THE POWER OF "NO"

We would be remiss if we failed to mention an extremely important component of any intervention or support we offer a child who is struggling. The child has complete and total veto power over any suggestion we make to help them. Quite simply, the child has the right to say, "NO", and we need to honor that. We need to operate from the perspective that the child knows what he needs, knows what he can tolerate and knows what may further activate him. If the child is opposed to a support or intervention, it's futile to attempt it. We should come from a place of respect and viewing the "child as expert" in knowing what he needs. When we can operate from that standpoint, we have a much better chance at helping the child.

A WORD OF CAUTION

We are not proposing that parents and teachers assume the role of therapists or traumatologists. However, we recognize the tremendous impact that "therapeutic" interventions have in a child's daily life. One does not have to be a therapist to have a therapeutic effect. In that vein, we recognize the importance of parents, teachers and caregivers having access to this knowledge, being trauma-informed and knowing how to best respond to trauma-induced behaviors. What's even more beautiful is that these techniques lend themselves to working with any child, traumatized or not. When we can respond with gentle, but powerful supports to struggling children, we help them in immeasurable ways.

RESOURCES:

Kohl, M.A. (1994). Preschool Art: It's the process, not the product

Lakes, K. D., & Hoyt, W. T. (2004). Promoting self-regulation through school-based martial arts training. *Applied Developmental Psychology*, 25, 283-302.

Malchiodi, C. (2006). Art Therapy Sourcebook

Malchiodi, C. & Perry, B. (2014) Creative Interventions with Traumatized Children

More tips from Wendy: Three Important Things Traumatized Kids Would Tell You If They Could

SAY

Would rubbing your back help you calm down?

BLOOM 50 Things To Say, Think, And Do With Anxious, Angry, and Over-the-Top Kids

SAY

Would you like to pound some clay until you feel better?

BLOOM 50 Things To Say, Think, And Do With Anxious, Angry, and Over-the-Top Kids

SAY

Rocking in the chair can help you feel better. Give it a try.

BLOOM 50 Things To Say, Think, And Do With Anxious, Angry, and Over-the-Top Kids

SAY

Want to blow some bubbles to help you calm down?

BLOOM 50 Things To Say, Think, And Do With Anxious, Angry, and Over-the-Top Kids

SAY

I'll walk around the block with you, if you'd like.

BLOOM 50 Things To Say, Think, And Do With Anxious, Angry, and Over-the-Top Kids

SAY

Let's shoot some hoops until you feel better.

BLOOM 50 Things To Say, Think, And Do With Anxious, Angry, and Over-the-Top Kids

SAY

Would like to draw me a picture that shows what's bothering you?

BLOOM 50 Things To Say, Think, And Do With Anxious, Angry, and Over-the-Top Kids

SAY

Would you like to draw what your (angry, sad, scared) feeling looks like?

BLOOM 50 Things To Say, Think, And Do With Anxious, Angry, and Over-the-Top Kids

SAY

We can just sit here quietly together.

BLOOM 50 Things To Say, Think, And Do With Anxious, Angry, and Over-the-Top Kids

SAY

BLOOM 50 Things To Say, Think, And Do With Anxious, Angry, and Over-the-Top Kids

SAY

BLOOM 50 Things To Say, Think, And Do With Anxious, Angry, and Over-the-Top Kids

SAY

BLOOM 50 Things To Say, Think, And Do With Anxious, Angry, and Over-the-Top Kids

THINK

This is a result of the trauma.

BLOOM 50 Things To Say, Think, And Do With Anxious, Angry, and Over-the-Top Kids

THINK

There is nothing wrong with this child. It's what happened to him that's the problem.

BLOOM 50 Things To Say, Think, And Do With Anxious, Angry, and Over-the-Top Kids

THINK

This child is not the problem. The problem is the problem.

BLOOM 50 Things To Say, Think, And Do With Anxious, Angry, and Over-the-Top Kids

THINK

This is triggering her. She is in a state of hyper-arousal.

BLOOM 50 Things To Say, Think, And Do With Anxious, Angry, and Over-the-Top Kids

THINK

This is the child's limbic brain speaking. There is no logical reasoning with it.

BLOOM 50 Things To Say, Think, And Do With Anxious, Angry, and Over-the-Top Kids

THINK

This behavior doesn't have to make sense to me.

BLOOM 50 Things To Say, Think, And Do With Anxious, Angry, and Over-the-Top Kids

THINK

The child may not be able to verbalize what is bothering her.

BLOOM 50 Things To Say, Think, And Do With Anxious, Angry, and Over-the-Top Kids

THINK

This child is reaching out for help.

BLOOM 50 Things To Say, Think, And Do With Anxious, Angry, and Over-the-Top Kids

THINK

I'm going to keep myself calm so I can help her be calm.

BLOOM 50 Things To Say, Think, And Do With Anxious, Angry, and Over-the-Top Kids

THINK

The first thing I try may not work. I will keep trying until we find a solution that helps.

BLOOM 50 Things To Say, Think, And Do With Anxious, Angry, and Over-the-Top Kids

THINK

I can help this child.

BLOOM 50 Things To Say, Think, And Do With Anxious, Angry, and Over-the-Top Kids

THINK

My goal is to help her calm down and feel safe.

BLOOM 50 Things To Say, Think, And Do With Anxious, Angry, and Over-the-Top Kids

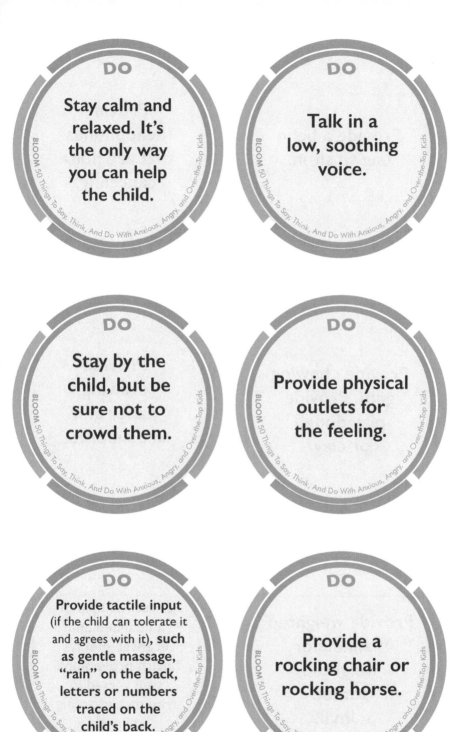

DO

Stay calm and relaxed. It's the only way you can help the child.

BLOOM 50 Things To Say, Think, And Do With Anxious, Angry, and Over-the-Top Kids

DO

Talk in a low, soothing voice.

BLOOM 50 Things To Say, Think, And Do With Anxious, Angry, and Over-the-Top Kids

DO

Stay by the child, but be sure not to crowd them.

BLOOM 50 Things To Say, Think, And Do With Anxious, Angry, and Over-the-Top Kids

DO

Provide physical outlets for the feeling.

BLOOM 50 Things To Say, Think, And Do With Anxious, Angry, and Over-the-Top Kids

DO

Provide tactile input (if the child can tolerate it and agrees with it), such as gentle massage, "rain" on the back, letters or numbers traced on the child's back.

BLOOM 50 Things To Say, Think, And Do With Anxious, Angry, and Over-the-Top Kids

DO

Provide a rocking chair or rocking horse.

BLOOM 50 Things To Say, Think, And Do With Anxious, Angry, and Over-the-Top Kids

DO

Provide a bean bag to sit in.

DO

Provide headphones that are noise canceling.

DO

Provide chewing gum. Provide play dough or clay.

DO

Provide drawing paper and art supplies.

DO

Provide weighted blankets or weighted stuffed animals.

DO

Enlist the help of a qualified and licensed mental health professional well versed in trauma and young children.

CHAPTER 11

Children and Grief

AN EARLY MOURNING

ittle Joshua's older brother, Henry, recently died from a congenital heart condition. Joshua is 4-years-old and Henry was six. Joshua's mom asks:

"Josh keeps pretend playing Henry's funeral over and over. He puts one of his stuffed animals in a shoe box and seems to play out what he remembers from the wake and funeral. It's really taking its toll on me. Not only am I grappling with my own horrific sense of grief; I'm watching Josh go through this and it breaks my heart all over again. I'm worried that this is a bad thing for him to continue to do. It seems like such a depressing way for him to play. Should I put my foot down and stop him from this type of play? Is this making things worse for him?"

It's something we'd like to not have to mention in the same sentence: children and grief. Yet, each year, hundreds of thousands of children will experience grief. Whether the loss is of a grandparent, parent, sibling, teacher or neighbor, children will feel the impact. They look to the adults in their lives to support them and help them through. The thing is, there is little written about grief in most parenting books. When grief becomes reality, parents have lots of questions.

Here's a similar concern from a mom, Tessa:

"My husband died after a two-year battle with cancer. The kids were very involved with his care and I believe they were as prepared as they possibly

could be for his death. While they cried after he died and during the funeral, I haven't seen much emotion in them since. Maybe they are moving forward and no longer feel the pain of his loss? I'm thinking I shouldn't cry in front of them at all, as it may be too troubling for them. Also, I'm wondering if they are trying to move forward, maybe I shouldn't bring up conversation with them about their dad."

Grief is not a disorder, illness or a sign of weakness. It is a necessity that is emotional, physical and spiritual. It's the price you pay for love. And the only way to healing sadness is to grieve.

– Earl Grollman

We'll get to some answers for these parents in a bit. In the meantime, let's take a look at some important concepts related to grieving children.

A grieving child is not a small adult. Their needs are vastly different than those of adults, and vary with each developmental phase.

HOW ARE CHILDREN OF DIFFERENT AGES AFFECTED BY GRIEF?

A child's developmental phase impacts how they experience grief. For our purposes, we are concerning ourselves with children from birth to 10 years of age. Here are a child's experiences, separated into three developmental stages according to *How Long Does the Sad Last: A Workbook for Grieving Children* by Wendy Young, LMSW, BCD. (Excerpted from "How Long Does the Sad Last: A Workbook for Grieving Children". Young, W., 2009, kidlutions.com).

Birth to Two: Infants and young children will react to the changes around them. They are perceptive to the feelings of others and "sense" the changes going on around them. Some infants and young children may respond by becoming difficult to soothe and feed and may seem "out of sorts".

Three to Five: Children at this age often think death is reversible. Magical thinking is common. Many children this age see cartoon characters "die" and pop back to life. It is important to explain to children that death is permanent, and that their loved one will not come back. Children will likely need many reminders of this just as they need many reminders when they are learning to tie shoes and zip coats.

Try to minimize your own frustration with having to tell them over and over again that death is forever.

Six to Ten: By this age, children understand that death is final. They begin to realize that they too can die. It is important to provide them with age-appropriate information. Children in this age range are media-savvy and are aware of murders and kidnappings committed against children. They need to be made to feel safe and protected. Children may question who will care for them if something happens to their caregivers. They need simple, honest information.

GRIEVING THROUGH THE YEARS

Another hallmark feature of grief for children, is how they tend to re-grieve the loss at each developmental phase. As their understanding of grief changes, their grief (and loss of the loved one) takes on a new meaning; a child in elementary school who lost a parent may have strong grief reactions as a teenager and as an adult. Grief doesn't go away, it just changes over time.

Grief is not something to "get over"; rather it is something to get through.

HOW DO I EXPLAIN DEATH TO MY CHILDREN?

Explaining death to a child can be difficult and overwhelming to the adults who love them. Know that keeping the truth from the child is not helpful, as some of us would want to believe. From the child's perspective, it is helpful to have a known and loving adult share the news with them about the death of a loved one. Following are some explanations that may be helpful in explaining death to your child.

EXPLAIN LIFE FIRST

When trying to explain death, it is often helpful to explain life, first. "We know somebody is living because they can breathe and eat and laugh and talk." "We can feel their heart beating in their chest or at a pulse point." You can demonstrate this for the child. "When people are alive, they can feel cold, hot, and pain."

THE BODY STOPS WORKING

Then explain to your child, "When somebody dies, they no longer breathe, eat, laugh or talk. We can no longer feel their heart beating in their chest or at a pulse point." "When somebody dies, they can no longer feel cold, hot, or pain. Their body has stopped working. They can no longer talk to us or hug us or do any of the things they used to do with us."

IT'S NOT YOUR FAULT

It's not your fault. "It is not your fault that your loved person has died. When somebody dies and their body stops working, there is nothing anybody can do to change it back".

Explain to your child, "There is nothing we could say or think that would make another person die." This is very important for children in the age group of about three to six-years-old because of their "magical thinking" and egocentricity. They may think, "I was mad at my sister for taking my doll and I wished she was never born. That's why she died." Or, "I told my mom I didn't like her anymore and I wish she would go away." Children in this age group should be reminded on several occasions that there is nothing they did to cause the death. Even though a child may not verbalize this fear, it is likely present.

USE PROPER TERMS

Refer to death directly. Use the words "died", "death", and "dead" in your explanations. While these words may seem harsh to us, we should avoid euphemisms like:

» "He passed away."
» "She is just sleeping."
» "He expired."
» "She is with the angels."
» "Grandpa is on a long trip."

These comments can confuse and even frighten children more than using the proper terms.

FOCUS ON FEELINGS

Flood of Feelings. When somebody dies, we have all kinds of feelings. We may feel sad, confused, angry, lonely, scared, worried, or a whole bunch of feelings at the same time. This is okay. We can talk about our feelings with each other. We can talk about our loved person who died.

DEATH IS UNIVERSAL

All living things will someday die. "Most people die when they are very old or sick, or get hurt very, very badly." Explain how this is not the kind of sick that we get when we have colds, flu, earaches, or sore throats. "Doctors have lots of very good medicines that can help us get better." "Almost all of the kinds of sickness that you and I will get can be fixed by doctors."

YOU DON'T HAVE TO DEAL WITH THIS ALONE

Tell your child, "I am here for you." Let your child know that you are there for them and that they can talk to you at any time about their feelings. Let your child know that you will ask them how they are doing, even if they don't talk to you about their feelings.

(Excerpted from "How Long Does the Sad Last: A Workbook for Grieving Children". Young, W., 2009, *kidlutions.com*)

BACK TO THE BEGINNING

Now, back to answering the questions from the beginning of this chapter:

JOSH

Joshua's need to continue to play out his older brother's wake and funeral is a typical response for kids his age. It can be difficult for parents and caregivers to witness, but it is part of the child's healing path.

THE IMPORTANCE OF PLAY

Play is how kids process and make sense of events which may be difficult for them to understand. "Playing it out" helps them process the event or situation. It is not recommended that adults try to stop this kind of play. You can support it by saying, "I can see you are thinking about what happened to Henry. You miss your brother." "You are sad he died. I am sad, too."

VALIDATE, VALIDATE, VALIDATE

You can then mention that sad feelings can last a while after someone we love dies. You can add, "We can talk about Henry whenever we'd like and we can give each other hugs when we are sad. We will get through this together." This validates his experiences and his feelings related to it.

GET MORE HELP WHEN NEEDED

This can all be very taxing on a parent who is on their own grief journey after the death of a child. It can be very helpful to enlist the help of a qualified and licensed mental health expert to support your child through this loss. They can also answer your questions directly and help you navigate the uncharted waters of grief.

TESSA'S FAMILY

Losing a parent is an incredibly difficult thing for a child, regardless of how long they had to prepare for the impending loss. Being the surviving parent of a child whose other parent has died is a challenge because you are dealing with your own grief, while simultaneously watching your child endure their grief journey. It can become overwhelming.

SHOULD A PARENT HIDE THEIR GRIEF?

The short answer is "NO". Parents do not have to hide their grief from their child. It is a common thought of parents, though. "I don't want to make things worse for my kids. I don't cry when they can see me. I don't want to keep reminding them of this loss."

Your kids are already thinking about the loss. Your tears are not a reminder about it. The thoughts, feelings, and experiences of grief are all with the child, whether or not they are talking to you about it.

CHILDREN NEED A MODEL FOR GRIEF

When parents elect to try to hide their grief, two significant things are lost for the child: A role model for how to grieve and validation that it is okay to be sad and move through that sadness by acknowledging one's feelings. Kids are often left wondering if their own tears are appropriate or if they should be kept to themselves. Sometimes, they may stifle their feelings in an attempt to protect other family members. They may find themselves wondering if they are normal, when nobody else in the family seems to be experiencing what they are.

In the past, we have worked with kids who have shared the following, "My mom doesn't really ever cry. I wonder why she doesn't still miss my dad. I miss him really bad. I try to never cry in front of her because I don't want to make her feel bad."

STRIKING A BALANCE

When you cry in front of your children during grief, it provides for them validation that sad feelings surround the loss of a loved one. It tells them it is okay to express those feelings. They learn those feelings will not destroy them and they do not last forever, even though it may feel that way at times. Allowing children to see your tears will not harm them. That said, it is best if more intense grief reactions like arm-flailing, teeth-gnashing and sobbing are saved for your alone moments. Striking a balance is the key. We know this is easier said than done. Find support in your adult family members, friends or enlist the help of a good therapist.

GRIEF WAVES

Grief can cause people to have moments of extreme sadness and desperation punctuated by moments of functioning fairly well. In this regard, grief tends to come on like waves. The grief can be overpowering, like a big crashing wave that pulls you under, followed by a period of stillness or calm, until another wave appears. This is true for both children and adults.

BEHAVIORAL ISSUES OF GRIEVING CHILDREN

REGRESSION

During periods of extreme stress, it is not unusual to see kids regressing to an earlier stage of development. This represents a step-backwards in time, when life felt safer. Children who have left tantrums behind may demonstrate a resurgence of this behavior. Potty-trained children may regress to needing diapers for a short time. Children who are drinking from a cup may ask for a bottle again. This can be expected for a short while, but if kids stay stuck in this backwards slide for months after a major loss, it is best to involve a behavioral health expert. If behaviors are very concerning to you, or interfere with the child's daily functioning, don't hesitate to seek professional care.

OTHER BEHAVIORAL CHANGES

A whole range of behavioral issues may surface for a bereaved child, including:

- » Eating changes: Too much or too little
- » Absent-mindedness

- » Trouble concentrating

- » Slipping grades, if school aged

- » Withdrawal from peers and others

- » Searching/crying out for the deceased

- » Sighing

- » Crying/Tantrums

- » Acting up, not listening

GRIEF IS PHYSICAL

Grief reactions are more than emotional. There are some very real physical reactions that occur as well.

Following are some of the reactions that may be experienced:

- » Fatigue/Low energy
- » Stomachaches
- » Headaches
- » Tight feeling in throat/chest
- » Shortness of breath
- » Weakness

HOW TO HELP A GRIEVING CHILD

What follows are things you can think, say and do that will help you help a grieving child.

WHAT YOU CAN **SAY**

It's hard to follow directions when your heart is full of sadness.

Would you like to draw a picture of how your sadness looks?

You're having really big feelings right now.

You're feeling really mad right now. It's okay to be mad. Let's go run around in the yard and see if it helps you feel better.

Want to jump up and down like popcorn popping and see if it helps shrink down your mad feelings?

Let's go bounce a ball really hard. That can help get your anger out.

Want to scream into a pillow? That can help shrink down mad or sad feelings.

Want to write a letter to your mom (dad, sister, brother, grandma) and tell them how much you miss them?

Want to have a pretend phone call with your mom (dad, sister, brother, grandma) and tell them what you want to say?

WHAT YOU CAN **THINK**

This is hard for him right now.

These behaviors are driven by grief.

He is not sure how to handle these big feelings on his own.

I can provide a stable, calm place for him to let go of all these overwhelming feelings.

He is doing the very best he can right now.

There is so much going on in his heart and in his head, it's leaking out as behavior.

He will get through this. I will help him.

Grief is so powerful. It's a challenge for adults. It's even harder for kids.

I'm trusting the process. He has to go through this to get to the other side.

WHAT YOU CAN **DO**

Allow the child to regress and provide support.

Provide plenty of physical contact (hugs, shoulder rubs, etc.).

Encourage children to play & have fun.

Allow safe ways to express feelings (drawing, coloring, building block towers and knocking them down, popping bubble wrap, stomping around like a BIG, ANGRY monster, ripping up old newspapers or magazines, gross motor activities, etc.).

Keep structure and routine. This is imperative.

Comfort a crying child. Allow tears and anger and every other feeling under the sun.

Tell the truth in a developmentally appropriate way.

Answer the child's questions.

If you don't know the answer, say so. Wonder together, out loud.

Include the child in rituals, memorials, planning.

Help the child create a memory box to save mementos of the loved one who is deceased.

CRAZY MIXED UP FEELINGS ACTIVITY

This activity can help kids recognize the many feelings that may surface in grief. It can lead to more discussion about how to handle said feelings.

NEEDED:

A clear drinking glass filled with water.

Food coloring of various colors.

PREPARATION:

Have the child identify some of the feelings associated with grief: sadness, anger, fear, shock, etc. Then have them match one feeling to each color you have. Write these down and create a key.

ACTIVITY:

Demonstrate for the child how many feelings are experienced during grief. Some anger (squirt the food coloring associated with anger into the water), some sadness (squirt the food coloring associated with sadness into the water), and so on.

DISCUSSION:

Discuss how many feelings are experienced during grief and that there are times when it seems they are all mixed together, and we aren't really sure what we are feeling.

Then discuss each feeling the child identified as associated with grief, and ask the child for ways to cope with that feeling. If the child is unable to identify ways to deal with said feelings, ask if he would like you to share some thoughts.

FOLLOW UP:

If the child is hesitant to discuss when you do this activity, feel free to bring it up in discussion at a future date, "Remember when we did the crazy mixed up feelings in a glass? I wonder if you have thought about that anymore. I have a few more ideas that might help when you get those BIG feelings. Want to hear them? I wonder what you think about them!"

THE MOST IMPORTANT THING TO REMEMBER

One of the most important things to remember about grieving children is that they can cope with it when provided the proper support and outlets. As a parent or adult caregiver, you have a tremendous opportunity to make a difference. The ideas we share here can really assist you in your quest to support children who grieve.

More resources for grieving children can be found at:

The Dougy Center: *dougy.org*

Ele's Place: *elesplace.org*

Childhood and Teen Grief Resources: *kidlutions.com*

SAY

It's hard to follow directions when your heart is full of sadness.

SAY

Would you like to draw a picture of how your sadness looks?

SAY

You're having really big feelings right now.

SAY

You're feeling really mad right now. It's okay to be mad. Let's go run around in the yard and see if it helps you feel better.

SAY

Want to jump up and down like popcorn popping and see if it helps shrink down your mad feelings?

SAY

Let's go bounce a ball really hard. That can help get your anger out.

SAY

Want to scream into a pillow? That can help shrink down mad or sad feelings.

BLOOM 50 Things To Say, Think, And Do With Anxious, Angry, and Over-the-Top Kids

SAY

Want to write a letter to your mom (dad, sister, brother, grandma) and tell them how much you miss them?

BLOOM 50 Things To Say, Think, And Do With Anxious, Angry, and Over-the-Top Kids

SAY

Want to have a pretend phone call with your mom (dad, sister, brother, grandma) and tell them what you want to say?

BLOOM 50 Things To Say, Think, And Do With Anxious, Angry, and Over-the-Top Kids

SAY

You're feeling really mad right now. It's okay to be mad. Let's go run around in the yard and see if it helps you feel better.

BLOOM 50 Things To Say, Think, And Do With Anxious, Angry, and Over-the-Top Kids

SAY

BLOOM 50 Things To Say, Think, And Do With Anxious, Angry, and Over-the-Top Kids

SAY

BLOOM 50 Things To Say, Think, And Do With Anxious, Angry, and Over-the-Top Kids

THINK

This is hard for him right now.

BLOOM 50 Things To Say, Think, And Do With Anxious, Angry, and Over-the-Top Kids

THINK

These behaviors are driven by grief.

BLOOM 50 Things To Say, Think, And Do With Anxious, Angry, and Over-the-Top Kids

THINK

He is not sure how to handle these big feelings on his own.

BLOOM 50 Things To Say, Think, And Do With Anxious, Angry, and Over-the-Top Kids

THINK

I can provide a stable, calm place for him to let go of all these overwhelming feelings.

BLOOM 50 Things To Say, Think, And Do With Anxious, Angry, and Over-the-Top Kids

THINK

He is doing the very best he can right now.

BLOOM 50 Things To Say, Think, And Do With Anxious, Angry, and Over-the-Top Kids

THINK

There is so much going on in his heart and in his head, it's leaking out as behavior.

BLOOM 50 Things To Say, Think, And Do With Anxious, Angry, and Over-the-Top Kids

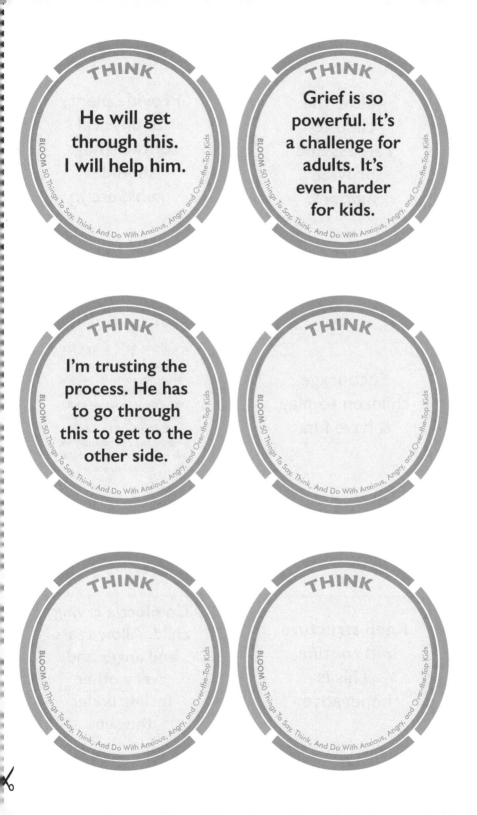

THINK

He will get through this. I will help him.

BLOOM 50 Things To Say, Think, And Do With Anxious, Angry, and Over-the-Top Kids

THINK

Grief is so powerful. It's a challenge for adults. It's even harder for kids.

BLOOM 50 Things To Say, Think, And Do With Anxious, Angry, and Over-the-Top Kids

THINK

I'm trusting the process. He has to go through this to get to the other side.

BLOOM 50 Things To Say, Think, And Do With Anxious, Angry, and Over-the-Top Kids

THINK

BLOOM 50 Things To Say, Think, And Do With Anxious, Angry, and Over-the-Top Kids

THINK

BLOOM 50 Things To Say, Think, And Do With Anxious, Angry, and Over-the-Top Kids

THINK

BLOOM 50 Things To Say, Think, And Do With Anxious, Angry, and Over-the-Top Kids

DO

Allow the child to regress and provide support.

BLOOM 50 Things To Say, Think, And Do With Anxious, Angry, and Over-the-Top Kids

DO

Provide plenty of physical contact (hugs, shoulder rubs, etc.).

BLOOM 50 Things To Say, Think, And Do With Anxious, Angry, and Over-the-Top Kids

DO

Encourage children to play & have fun.

BLOOM 50 Things To Say, Think, And Do With Anxious, Angry, and Over-the-Top Kids

DO

Allow safe ways to express feelings (drawing, coloring, building block towers and knocking them down, popping bubble wrap, stomping around like a BIG, ANGRY monster, ripping up old newspapers or magazines, gross motor activities, etc.).

BLOOM 50 Things To Say, Think, And Do With Anxious, Angry, and Over-the-Top Kids

DO

Keep structure and routine. This is imperative.

BLOOM 50 Things To Say, Think, And Do With Anxious, Angry, and Over-the-Top Kids

DO

Comfort a crying child. Allow tears and anger and every other feeling under the sun.

BLOOM 50 Things To Say, Think, And Do With Anxious, Angry, and Over-the-Top Kids

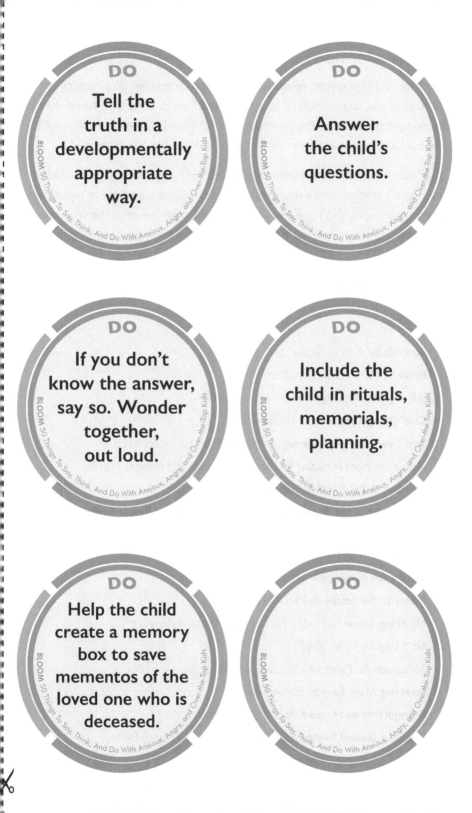

DO
Tell the truth in a developmentally appropriate way.

BLOOM 50 Things To Say, Think, And Do With Anxious, Angry, and Over-the-Top Kids

DO
Answer the child's questions.

BLOOM 50 Things To Say, Think, And Do With Anxious, Angry, and Over-the-Top Kids

DO
If you don't know the answer, say so. Wonder together, out loud.

BLOOM 50 Things To Say, Think, And Do With Anxious, Angry and Over-the-Top Kids

DO
Include the child in rituals, memorials, planning.

BLOOM 50 Things To Say, Think, And Do With Anxious, Angry, and Over-the-Top Kids

DO
Help the child create a memory box to save mementos of the loved one who is deceased.

BLOOM 50 Things To Say, Think, And Do With Anxious, Angry, and Over-the-Top Kids

DO

BLOOM 50 Things To Say, Think, And Do With Anxious, Angry, and Over-the-Top Kids

SO LONG, FOR NOW

Well you did it! You read, reviewed and even practiced over 50 strategies aimed at helping you, your family and your child's teachers to build brain-based skills in anxious, angry and over-the top children. With your help we can move a nation from a focus on consequences to a focus on skill building. We thank you!

It is our honor to have taken this journey with you to help your children, particularly children who experience intense emotions, learn how to metabolize their experiences. We hope that you enjoy and make use of all the new words, thoughts and feelings offered in Bloom. Please let us know how it is going for you. We care.

MORE RESOURCES FOR YOU

BOOKS

Backtalk by Audrey Ricker

Brave by Marjie Braun Knudsen

Building Moral Intelligence by Michele Borba

Chief Daddy Officer by Chris Efessiou

Cool Down and Work Through Anger by Cheri J. Meiners M.Ed.

Hands Are Not For Hitting by Elizabeth Verdick and Marieka Heinlen

If I Have to Tell You One More Time by Amy McCready

In the Spirit of the Studio: Learning from the Atelier of Reggio Emilia by Lella Gandini et al.

Inspired Children (Ed.) Rosina McAlpine

Kissing The Mirror by Marlaine Cover

Nanny to the Rescue by Michelle LaRowe

No Biting, Louise by Margie Palatini and Matthew Reinhart

No Biting! By Karen Katz

Parachutes for Parents by Bobbi Sandoz-Merrill

Parenting Made Easy by Sue Atkins

Peaceful Parents Happy Kids by Laura Markham

Raising a Sensory Smart Child by Lindsey Biel and Nancy Peske

Raising Cain by Dan Kindlon and Michael Thompson

Raising Your Spirited Child by Mary Sheedy Kurcinka

Relax Kids: The Wishing Star: 52 Magical Meditations for Children by Marneta Viegas

Screamfree Parenting by Hal Runkel

Siblings Without Rivalry: How to Help Your Children Live Together So You Can Live Too by Adele Faber and Elaine Mazlish

The You We Adore by Valerie Westfall

Two Thousand Kisses A Day by LR Knost

Stop Reacting and Start Responding by Sharon Silver

Stress-Free Potty Training: A Commonsense Guide to Finding the Right Approach for Your Child by Sara Au and Peter Stavinoha

Teaching Kids to Be Good People by Annie Fox

Teaching Montessori in the Home by Elizabeth Hainstock

Teenage as a Second Language by Barbara Greenberg and Jennifer Powell-Lunder

Teeth are Not for Biting by Elizabeth Verdick and Marieka Heinlen

The Big Book of Parenting Solutions by Michele Borba, EdD

The Bipolar Disorder Survival Guide, Second Edition: What You and Your Family Need to Know by David Miklowitz, PhD

The Blossom Method by Vivien Sabel

The Boy Who Was Raised as a Dog by Bruce Perry, MD, PhD

The Explosive Child by Ross Greene, PhD

The Family Coach Method by Lynne Kenney, PsyD

The Parents Toolkit by Naomi Richards

The Teen Years - Don't Get Mad - Get Through - A Parent's Guide to Surviving the Teenage Years Without Tearing Your Hair Out by Sarah Newton

The Whole Brain Child by Dan Siegel, MD and Tina Payne Bryson

What to Do When You Worry Too Much: A Kid's Guide to Overcoming Anxiety by Dawn Huebner

Wits End by Sue Scheff

WEBSITES

Braininsightsonline.com

Deeanddoo.com

Flip2bfit.com

Littlejots.com

Karismakidz.co.uk

Kiboomu.com

Kimochis.com

Momtalkradio.com

Movingsmart.biz

NAEYC.org

Nightmarenibbler.com

Relaxkids.com

Sayinggoodbye.org

Sparkpe.org

Teachpreschool.org

Thecoffeeklatch.com

Theconfidentmom.com

Theteendoc.com

Zerotothree.org

A WORD OF THANKS FROM LYNNE

When a parent pursues a dream, the entire family is an integral part of the journey, giving, supporting, encouraging and participating. With the warmest of hearts I wish to thank my husband Rick and daughters Olivia and Alexis for their patience and generosity as they made their own breakfast, folded their own laundry and provided editorial input over and over again as we created Bloom. Many of my colleagues and mentors have also given to the spirit of this book. The wisdom of Diana Vigil, Shea Schwartz, Paul Beljan, Paul Kelly, Catherine Dees, Abby Dees, Karen Saywitz, Ron Schouten, Raun Melmed, Beth Onufrak, Deb McNelis, Annie Fox, Sue Atkins and more is weaved within the tapestry of the Bloom philosophy. This philosophy grew over a lifetime of learning and engagement, with many people wiser than I. I also wish to thank my parents and brothers, who have parented with us as a village, allowing our children to know love in every corner of their lives. Our publisher, Megan Hunter, of Unhooked Books sought to publish a revolutionary book that gives parents and teachers the words to shift a generation. To you, Megan we are enthusiastically grateful for your creativity and courage.

A WORD OF THANKS FROM WENDY

It takes tenacity to write a book and it requires the support of an entire family. Thanks to my husband, Jim, who has provided untiring support in every single one of my endeavors, over the course of almost three decades. You help make it all possible. To my children, James, Gabrielle and Warner, for teaching me so much about life, love, parenting and who make me want to be a better person in every way. You are my greatest proof that the approach to parenting detailed in this book is indeed powerful. Thanks a million times over to my own parents, James and Judy Warner, under whose roof I always knew love. And to my siblings, Jim and Julie, for sharing this incredible journey of life. Gratitude to David Cochrane and Jean Jablonski, administrators at Family Forum, Inc., who allowed me to lead their programs' behavioral and mental health components for over a decade, utilizing the BLOOM approach, before it even had a name. I am grateful for every early childhood teacher in their programs who are on the front lines every day, and have embraced the tenets in this book. Thanks to teachers like Jonelle France, Sherri Nyquist and Dawn Wolfe, whose magical way of being with kids touched my family personally, and to the hundreds of other teachers who work magic in their classrooms and the hearts of their students on a daily basis. Thanks to my early mentors and supervisors, Cara Frappier, Cheryl Olden and Alice Walker. I am indebted, also, to the countless families and individuals who gave me permission to share a portion of their journeys. You are all a part of my heart. I am eternally beholden to Dr. Lynne Kenney, and our thousands of hours of conversation, texts, emails and phone calls, all of which culminated in BLOOM. Finally, I am forever obliged to Megan Hunter of Unhooked Books, for her belief in BLOOM and for her courage in backing an innovative and progressive parenting book. She is a visionary in her field and without her support, this book would still be but a dream.

ABOUT THE AUTHORS

Lynne Kenney, Psy.D, is a mother of two, a practicing pediatric psychologist in Scottsdale, AZ, and the author of *The Family Coach Method*. She has advanced fellowship training in forensic psychology and developmental pediatric psychology from Massachusetts General Hospital/Harvard Medical School and Harbor-UCLA/UCLA Medical School. Her content has appeared in Parenting, Parents, Success, Real Simple, People Magazine and more. Dr. Lynne's current interest is enhancing children's math and thinking skills (ages 6-12) using movement with Play Math and Move2Think. ***www.lynnekenney.com***

Facebook: facebook.com/DrLynneKenney
Pinterest: pinterest.com/lynnekenney/
Twitter: twitter.com/DrLynneKenney
Website: lynnekenney.com

Wendy Young, LMSW, BCD, is the mom of three, an award-winning child and family therapist and an Early Childhood Mental Health Consultant. She graduated Summa Cum Laude from Michigan State University's School of Social Work and is the Clinical Director of Comprehensive Counseling & Consulting, LLC. Her writing has appeared in several magazines, including: Parenting, Family Fun and Woman's World. Her expertise has been utilized in several books and online publications. She is the behavioral health expert for Momtourage.com and resides in Michigan's Upper Peninsula. ***www.kidlutions.com***

Facebook: facebook.com/kidlutions
Pinterest: pinterest.com/kidlutions/
Twitter: twitter.com/Kidlutions
Website: kidlutions.com

| So Long, For Now

All of the colorful mantra cards at the end of each chapter can be copied directly from this book or you may download and print them directly from our website at:

WWW.UNHOOKEDBOOKS.COM